The MAJESTY of GOD'S SON

Insight for Living
Bible Study Guide

From the Bible-teaching ministry of
Charles R. Swindoll

INSIGHT FOR LIVING

Chuck graduated in 1963 from Dallas Theological Seminary, where he now serves as the school's fourth president, helping to prepare a new generation of men and women for the ministry. Chuck has served in pastorates in three states: Massachusetts, Texas, and California, including almost twenty-three years at the First Evangelical Free Church in Fullerton, California. He is currently senior pastor of Stonebriar Community Church in Frisco, Texas, north of Dallas. His sermon messages have been aired over radio since 1979 as the *Insight for Living* broadcast. A best-selling author, Chuck has written numerous books and booklets on many subjects.

Based on the outlines and transcripts of Charles R. Swindoll's sermons, the study guide text was developed and written by the Educational Ministries Department at Insight for Living.

Editor in Chief:
Cynthia Swindoll

Study Guide Writer:
Jason Shepherd

Senior Editor and Assistant Writer:
Wendy Peterson

Assistant Editor:
Glenda Schalahta

Editors:
Christina Grimstad
Karla Lenderink

Copy Editor:
Marco Salazar

Rights and Permissions:
Julie Meredith

Text Designer:
Gary Lett

Graphic System Administrator:
Bob Haskins

Director, Communications Division:
John Norton

Print Production Manager:
Don Bernstein

Project Coordinator:
Jennifer Hubbard

Printer:
Sinclair Printing Company

Unless otherwise identified, all Scripture references are from the New American Standard Bible, updated edition, copyright © The Lockman Foundation 1960, 1962, 1963, 1968, 1971, 1972, 1973, 1975, 1977, 1995. Used by permission. Scripture taken from the Holy Bible, New International Version, Copyright © 1973, 1978, 1984 International Bible Society, used by permission of Zondervan Bible Publishers [NIV]. The other translation cited is *The Message*.

An effort has been made to locate sources and obtain permission where necessary for the quotations used in this book. In the event of any unintentional omission, a modification will gladly be incorporated in future printings.

ISBN 1-57972-326-8

Printed in the United States of America.

COVER DESIGN: Alex Pasieka

COVER PHOTOGRAPH: Bob Haskins

CONTENTS

INTRODUCTION

*M*ajesty. *Webster's* says this word describes something of "greatness or splendor of quality or character." When applied to Jesus, *majesty* only begins to define our Savior. Jesus indeed exhibited majestic greatness and splendor in His quality and character, but can we use a word to describe Him that we also use on a Van Gogh painting or a Fabergé egg? It hardly seems right.

That's why I hope you'll open the pages of this study guide and read every word. I want you to see how Jesus distinguishes Himself from all other things we might call "majestic." I want you to see Him:

- In His preincarnate state, acting as Co-creator of the world with His Father.

- Offering the abundant life and much-needed rest to weary people.

- Hanging on a cross bearing the sins of the world.

- Rising from the dead as proof that the payment for sin was accepted by the Father.

- Encouraging and challenging His followers to make disciples until He returns.

In the end, I hope the majesty of Jesus will fill you with wonder and praise and draw you closer to the One who loves you more than you'll ever know.

Chuck Swindoll

PUTTING TRUTH
INTO ACTION

K nowledge apart from application falls short of God's desire for His children. He wants us to apply what we learn so that we will change and grow. This study guide was prepared with these goals in mind. As you go through the following pages, we hope your desire to discover biblical truth will grow as your understanding of God's Word increases, and that you will be encouraged to apply what you've learned.

To assist you in your study, we've included a section called 🐾 **Living Insights** at the end of each lesson. These exercises will challenge you to study further and to think of specific ways to put your discoveries into action.

There are many ways to use this guide—in personal devotions, group studies, discussions with friends and family, and Sunday school classes. And, of course, it's an ideal study aid when you're listening to its corresponding *Insight for Living* radio series.

To benefit most from this study guide, we would encourage you to consider it a spiritual journal. That's why we've included space in the **Living Insights** for recording your thoughts and discoveries. We hope you'll return to those sections often for review and encouragement as you continue to grow in your walk with Christ.

Insight for Living

The MAJESTY of GOD'S SON

Chapter 1

THE IDENTITY OF DEITY

Selected Scriptures

Who is Jesus?

Most people in the world don't know much about Him. If we were to ask people on the street, we'd hear responses like: "Jesus was a great moral teacher," or, "He founded a religion," or, "He was a good man who was kind to kids." Even some who have attended church since childhood couldn't give more than a vague answer filled with qualifiers such as, "Some people say Jesus was a . . . but others think He was more of a . . ."

These responses, though inadequate and inaccurate, raise a crucial question: Why is it important to have an accurate understanding of who Jesus was and is? After all, what difference does it make what we think of a man who lived two thousand years ago?

The Bible teaches that it makes a big difference! It tells us that the eternal destiny of every human being depends on Him (see John 3:16). In order to be spared from the wrath and judgment of God, a person must believe in Him (see Rom. 8:1). He is the only One who can save us from eternal damnation and grant us entry into heaven.

What exactly must we believe about Him? Many people believe He was a great moral teacher who founded a religion. Both of these statements are true, but they're not enough to constitute a faith that saves.

This chapter will identify the essential characteristics of Jesus' identity. In order to exercise a faith in Him that will save us, we must first know and believe these things about Him. Before we look at them, though, let's examine some passages that reveal how Jesus was misunderstood and misidentified, even in His own day.

Questions about His Identity

Our society's lack of knowledge of who Jesus really is could be chalked up to His having lived so long ago. Jesus' contemporaries, however, couldn't hide behind any such excuse. Their nearness to Him, unfortunately, didn't help. They ignored His credentials just as much as we do today.

From Religious Leaders

The religious leaders of the day—the Pharisees, Sadducees, and scribes—should have identified Jesus more quickly than anyone else. They knew the Scriptures. They had read all the prophecies. Yet when they saw Him teaching in the temple one day, they puzzled over His identity.

> One day He was teaching; and there were some Pharisees and teachers of the law sitting there, who had come from every village of Galilee and Judea and from Jerusalem; and the power of the Lord was present for Him to perform healing. And some men were carrying on a bed a man who was paralyzed; and they were trying to bring him in and to set him down in front of Him. But not finding any way to bring him in because of the crowd, they went up on the roof and let him down through the tiles with his stretcher, into the middle of the crowd, in front of Jesus. Seeing their faith, He said, "Friend, your sins are forgiven you." The scribes and the Pharisees began to reason, saying, "Who is this man who speaks blasphemies? Who can forgive sins, but God alone?" (Luke 5:17–21)

Not only were the religious leaders baffled by Jesus, but they became highly offended by Him as well. What a shame! The men who should have been the first to identify and embrace Jesus chose instead to hate Him.

From Civic Leaders

Civic leaders, in order to maintain peace and order, keep their fingers on the pulse of activities pumping in and out of their communities. Herod was no exception. He was a master of getting information on the "who" and "what" of his region. Yet when it came to Jesus, he, like the religious leaders, remained in the dark.

> Now Herod the tetrarch heard of all that was happening; and he was greatly perplexed, because it was said by some that John had risen from the dead, and by some that Elijah had appeared, and by others that one of the prophets of old had risen again. Herod said, "I myself had John beheaded; but who is this man about whom I hear such things?" And he kept trying to see Him. (Luke 9:7–9)

Herod's network of informants came up with mixed answers, which made Jesus a wrench in Herod's well-oiled information machine. This crafty politician was confounded when faced with this mysterious man named Jesus.

From People in His Hometown

If you can't rely on the people from your hometown to know who you are, on whom can you rely? Jesus might have been asking Himself this very question after He traveled back to Nazareth to minister to His hometown folks.

> Jesus went out from there and came into His hometown; and His disciples followed Him. When the Sabbath came, He began to teach in the synagogue; and the many listeners were astonished, saying, "Where did this man get these things, and what is this wisdom given to Him, and such miracles as these performed by His hands? Is not this the carpenter, the son of Mary, and brother of James and Joses and Judas and Simon? Are not His sisters here with us?" And they took offense at Him. (Mark 6:1–3)

Jesus couldn't catch a break! Even the people who had watched Him grow up were rejecting Him. Their familiarity with Him bred contempt rather than faith.

From His Own Students

Jesus was quickly becoming a completely misunderstood man. But not all hope was gone; He still had His disciples, those closest to Him and they wouldn't let Him down. Or would they?

> On that day, when evening came, He said to them, "Let us go over to the other side [of the sea]." Leaving the crowd, they took Him along with them

in the boat, just as He was; and other boats were with Him. And there arose a fierce gale of wind, and the waves were breaking over the boat so much that the boat was already filling up. Jesus Himself was in the stern, asleep on the cushion; and they woke Him and said to Him, "Teacher do You not care that we are perishing?" And He got up and rebuked the wind and said to the sea, "Hush, be still." And the wind died down and it became perfectly calm. And He said to them, "Why are you afraid? How is it that you have no faith?" They became very much afraid and said to one another, "Who then is this, that even the wind and the sea obey Him?" (Mark 4:35–41)

You guessed it—the disciples failed Him too. And they not only failed to recognize His true identity, but they actually feared Him!

Isn't it amazing that people who actually saw Jesus failed to recognize Him for who He was? They could see Him with their own eyes as He lived, taught, and performed miracles before them in the flesh. But you know what? We, too, have a living record of Jesus. The words and works of His earthly life still live in the Bible, which chronicles them for all to see.

Let's not miss what's in front of *our* faces. Instead, let's direct our full attention to what Scripture has to say about who Jesus is.

The Facts about His Deity

A great place to learn about Jesus' true identity is the Gospel of John. In the first chapter, John reveals an essential element of Jesus—His deity. Jesus Christ was, and is, God. He is the Second Person of the Trinity, ruling with the Father and the Holy Spirit. In this position, Christ fulfills several roles, all of which are extensions of His deity.

He Is God's "Logos"

First, He is the *Logos* of God:

> In the beginning was the Word, and the Word was with God, and the Word was God. (John 1:1)

The Greeks used the term *word*, *logos*, to describe speech—the expression of someone's thoughts. As the *Logos* of God, Jesus acted

4

as the physical expression of God to humanity. He revealed God's mind to us.[1]

John states three facts about this *Logos* of God. First, He existed "in the beginning." This phrase obviously plays on the first verse of Genesis, "In the beginning God created the heavens and the earth." Through this wordplay, John reveals the deity of Jesus by showing that He existed before His physical, human birth. In fact, He existed before creation, just as the Father and the Holy Spirit did.

Second, the *Logos* was "*with* God." This phrase describes the personal character of the Word—He exists "in the closest possible connection with the Father."[2] The two are not exactly the same, but they are one in nature.[3]

Finally, the *Logos* "*was* God." This third description reaches the highest point of John's affirmation of Jesus' deity. Nothing more needs to be said. Jesus is divine; as the *Logos* of God, He is God.

He Is Our Creator

Interestingly, both the Greek and Jewish concepts of *logos* "conveyed the idea of beginnings—the world began through the Word (see Genesis 1:3ff., where the expression occurs repeatedly)."[4] John certainly had this idea in mind when he used the term to describe Jesus. However, he didn't rely on merely a vague connotation to identify Jesus as the Creator of the world; he came out and stated it:

> All things came into being through Him, and apart from Him nothing came into being that has come into being. (John 1:3)

Everything that exists owes its existence to Christ. Notice, however, that John does not say creation was made "by" Him but "through" Him. Putting it this way safeguards the truth that the Father is the source of all that exists. Christ acts as the agent through whom the Father created.[5] "All creation," sums up Edwin

---

1. Bruce B. Barton and others, *John*, Life Application Bible Commentary series (Wheaton, Ill.: Tyndale House Publishers, 1993), p. 3.

2. Leon Morris, *The Gospel according to John*, rev. ed., The New International Commentary on the New Testament series (Grand Rapids, Mich.: William B. Eerdmans Publishing Co., 1995), p. 68.

3. Morris, *The Gospel according to John*, p. 68.

4. Barton and others, *John*, p. 3.

5. Morris, *The Gospel according to John*, p. 71.

Blum, "was made by the Word in relation with the Father and the Spirit."[6] Or as the apostle Paul put it:

> [Jesus] is the image of the invisible God. . . . For by Him all things were created, both in the heavens and on earth, visible and invisible, whether thrones or dominions or rulers or authorities—all things have been created through Him and for Him. He is before all things, and in Him all things hold together. (Col. 1:15–17)

He Is Our Life

Christ not only created physical life, but He also gives spiritual life.

> In Him was life, and the life was the Light of men. (John 1:4)

Jesus Christ gives spiritual life to those who believe in Him. The Greek term for *life, zoe,* always describes the divine, eternal life in John's Gospel.[7] Jesus Himself used this specific term during the Last Supper when He told His disciples, "I am the way, and the truth, and the life; no one comes to the Father but through Me" (14:6).

As the "Light of men," Christ seeks to dispel the darkness (1:4–5). Darkness in the Bible represents ignorance, sin, death, and separation from God.[8] As the antithesis of these things, Jesus Christ is our Light and Life.

He Is Our Savior

Finally, John identifies the role that means the most to us.

> But as many as received Him, to them He gave the right to become children of God, even to those who believe in His name. (v. 12)

Jesus Christ is our Savior. To receive Him as such means to believe that He lived and died to pay for our sins so that we might receive forgiveness and eternal life with God. When we believe in

6. Edwin A. Blum, "John," in *The Bible Knowledge Commentary*, New Testament edition, ed. John F. Walvoord and Roy B. Zuck (Colorado Springs, Colo.: Chariot Victor Publishing, 1983), p. 271.

7. Barton and others, *John*, p. 5.

8. Blum, "John," pp. 271–72.

Him, we accept the truth that He sacrificed Himself on our behalf—He took our place and bore God's wrath against sin for us. As a result, we become God's children and obtain the free gift of eternal life. This gift is free, but we must express faith in Christ to receive it.

What difference does it make, then, what we think of Jesus? As we've seen, it makes all the difference. Who was Jesus—merely a great moral teacher or the founder of a religion? Or was He actually God? Decide for yourself, but think carefully. Your eternal destiny rides on the choice you make.

Living Insights

Like it or not, you've come to a fork in the road. You've been presented with the truth about Jesus Christ. He was, and is, God. He created you, and now He offers you forgiveness of your sin and the free gift of eternal life. Which road will you take? Will you bow in repentance and receive His offer, or will you turn away and refuse to acknowledge Him?

God is calling you into His family, if you want to trust in Christ, the process is not complicated. Romans 10:9 says, "If you confess with your mouth Jesus as Lord, and believe in your heart that God raised Him from the dead, you will be saved." If you desire to be saved, all you have to do is pray to God. Here's a sample prayer:

> Dear Jesus,
> Thank You for dying on the cross for my sin. I believe Your death was meant to bring me salvation. I trust in You as my Savior. Thank You for forgiving my sin and giving me new life. Amen.

If you express the thoughts of this prayer, you can rest assured in the promise of Romans 10:9 that "you will be saved." You are now a Christian as it is defined by the Bible. But don't keep this truth hidden. Tell someone who you know is a Christian, and start attending a Bible-teaching church.

Chapter 2

A RELATIONSHIP, A COURTSHIP, A MIRACLE

Selected Scriptures

"Cleanliness is next to godliness" goes the old proverb. Sometimes, though, cleanliness is not always the best thing, as the discoverer of penicillin, Sir Alexander Fleming, found out.

> Fleming's discovery of penicillin was made by accident when a speck of dust happened to land on an uncovered culture plate. Touring a modern research laboratory some years later, he observed with interest the sterile, dust-free, air-conditioned environment in which the scientists worked. "What a pity you did not have a place like this to work in," said his guide. "Who can tell what you might have discovered in such surroundings!"
>
> "Not penicillin," remarked Fleming with a smile.[1]

Sometimes a little messiness can make all the difference! This is especially true in relationships. How many of our marriages, friendships, and relationships with our kids glide along without a hitch? Misunderstandings mark our way, and human foibles make us a lot less like "Martha Stewart perfect" and a lot more like "Erma Bombeck messy," don't they? But when we work through them, our love and appreciation for one another becomes so much richer.

You know what? Jesus' family was messy too. Joseph and Mary's betrothal was turned upside down by God's unexpected "speck of dust." But it was within this messy environment that God brought about a great miracle . . . and the greatest gift to the world.

The Mess

Christ's birth took place in less-than-ideal circumstances. He was born in a stable, laid in a feeding trough, and wrapped in

---

1. Clifton Fadiman, gen. ed., *The Little, Brown Book of Anecdotes* (Boston, Mass.: Little, Brown and Co., 1985), p. 210.

swaddling cloths—hardly the sterile environment of a hospital or the cozy surroundings of a home. The "mess," however, started long before Mary and Joseph ever made their way to Bethlehem. It all started in a city called Nazareth.

The Town

Joseph and Mary lived in Nazareth, a small city in the Galilee region (Luke 1:26–27). As natives of this town, their future Son would be called "Jesus of Nazareth" (see Matt. 26:71; Mark 1:24; Luke 18:37; John 1:45; Acts 10:38). What was Nazareth like? Many people turn to the words of Jesus' disciple Nathanael for a clue.

> Philip found Nathanael and said to him, "We have found Him of whom Moses in the Law and also the Prophets wrote—Jesus of Nazareth, the son of Joseph." Nathanael said to him, "Can any good thing come out of Nazareth?" Philip said to him, "Come and see." (John 1:45–46)

Why would Nathanael ask such a sarcastic question? Scholars and commentators give us a variety of views, some conflicting, of what Nazareth was like. Merrill Unger and a few others believe that Nathanael's use of the word *good* "must be taken in an ethical sense and that the people of Nazareth had a bad name among their neighbors for irreligion or some laxity of morals."[2] *The IVP Bible Background Commentary*, however, presents Nazareth as a "very traditional, orthodox town; priests later considered it ritually clean enough to move there."[3] And the *New Bible Dictionary: Second Edition* claims that since Nazareth "lay close enough to several main trade-routes for easy contact with the outside world" and was kind of a frontier town, it had an independent spirit that "led to the scorn in which Nazareth was held by strict Jews."[4]

The majority of resources steer away from making any conclusions about Nazareth's overall character, so it seems best for us to

---

2. Merrill F. Unger, *The New Unger's Bible Dictionary*, rev. ed., ed. R. K. Harrison (Chicago, Ill.: Moody Press, 1988), p. 907.

3. Craig S. Keener, *The IVP Bible Background Commentary: New Testament* (Downers Grove, Ill.: InterVarsity Press, 1993), p. 267.

4. J. W. Charley, "Nazareth," in *New Bible Dictionary: Second Edition.*, rev. ed. (1982; reprint, Downers Grove, Ill.: InterVarsity Press, 1991), p. 819.

avoid speculating about it too. Instead, we're safe in noting that Nazareth was:

- located on a hillside in a high, secluded valley,

- probably overshadowed by a very large city nearby, Sepphoris, "which rivaled Tiberias [John 6:23] for its urban Greek character in Jewish Galilee,"[5]

- not far from international trade routes, making it secluded in its valley but not isolated from the outside world,

- small in size and population and rather obscure,

- not mentioned in the Old Testament or its prophecies regarding the Messiah.

Nathanael's zinger against Nazareth, then, simply could have sprung from a rivalry between that town and his small town of Cana, which was not far away.[6] Or it could reveal what so many of the Jews of Jesus' day struggled with: their expectations. Would a king come from such an unimportant place as Nazareth? And anyway, the Messiah was supposed to come from Bethlehem, as the prophet Micah foretold:

> "But as for you, Bethlehem Ephrathah,
> Too little to be among the clans of Judah,
> From you One will go forth for Me to be a ruler
>   in Israel.
> His goings forth are from long ago,
> From the days of eternity." (Mic. 5:2)

This prophecy is clear: The Savior could not come from anywhere but Bethlehem. Mary and Joseph, though, are living in Nazareth. Things are getting a little messy.

The Courtship

Mary and Joseph's relationship seems puzzling to those of us who live in modern, Western societies. In the days prior to Christ's birth, the Bible says these young teens were "betrothed" (Matt. 1:18).

---

5. Keener, *The IVP Bible Background Commentary*, p. 267.

6. Leon Morris, *The Gospel according to John* (1971; reprint, Grand Rapids, Mich.: William B. Eerdmans Publishing Co., 1984), p. 165.

Many of us take that to mean they were engaged. But during this same time, the Bible describes Joseph as Mary's husband (Matt. 1:19). How can that be? Biblical historian Ralph Gower explains:

> Once the arrangement to marry was entered into, there was a betrothal that was more binding than the engagement in contemporary society. . . .
> . . . The betrothal could be broken only by a legal transaction (in effect, a divorce), and the ground for such termination was adultery (see Deuteronomy 22:24). Betrothal lasted for about twelve months, during which the home was to be prepared by the groom, and the wedding clothes would be prepared by the bride. The bride's family would prepare the wedding festivities.[7]

Although Joseph and Mary are not yet married, they are involved in a relationship that cannot be dissolved on a whim. Joseph is building a home. Mary's mother, father, and any siblings she has are making preparations for the wedding celebration. Mary herself is choosing fabrics and sewing her elaborate dress. The families of these two young people have committed them to a legally and socially binding relationship. This is why Joseph is already called her husband, and this is why the "mess" is about to become messier.

The Problem

Mary must feel such anticipation during this promising time of her life! A teenage girl full of dreams, she looks through hope-filled eyes at the life that lies before her. God, though, with one stroke of His sovereign brush, adds an odd color to her dreams. An angel, Gabriel, appears to Mary with some glorious yet unsettling news.

> And coming in, he said to her, "Greetings, favored one! The Lord is with you." But she was very perplexed at this statement, and kept pondering what kind of salutation this was. The angel said to her, "Do not be afraid, Mary; for you have found favor with God. And behold, you will conceive in your

---

7. Ralph Gower, *The New Manners and Customs of Bible Times* (Chicago, Ill.: Moody Press, 1987), p. 65.

womb and bear a son, and you shall name Him Jesus. He will be great and will be called the Son of the Most High; and the Lord God will give Him the throne of His father David; and He will reign over the house of Jacob forever, and His kingdom will have no end." (Luke 1:28–33)

Can you imagine Mary's thoughts? "Great news, Lord, but *terrible* timing!" From her perspective, the Lord could not have bestowed on her a greater honor, but she isn't married yet. So she asks the angel,

"How can this be, since I am a virgin?" The angel answered and said to her, "The Holy Spirit will come upon you, and the power of the Most High will overshadow you; and for that reason the holy Child shall be called the Son of God." (vv. 34–35)

To encourage her that God could really create life in her, the angel adds,

"And behold, even your relative Elizabeth has also conceived a son in her old age; and she who was called barren is now in her sixth month. For nothing will be impossible with God." (vv. 36–37)

A model of faith for us, Mary tells the angel, "Behold, the bondslave of the Lord; may it be done to me according to your word" (v. 38). Then she hurries to Elizabeth's house in Judah, where she receives a joyous greeting. Dwight Pentecost describes the scene:

When one came unexpectedly and sought admission to the household, those within would inquire about the identity of the one seeking admission. When Mary identified herself, Luke recorded, "Elizabeth was filled with the Holy Spirit" (Luke 1:41). She becomes a prophetess who, under the control of the Holy Spirit, made a prophetic utterance. She cried, "Blessed are you among women, and blessed is the child you will bear" (v. 42). . . . Thus Elizabeth proclaimed that Mary was to be the mother of the Messiah. . . .

. . . This meeting also confirmed to Mary that God would fulfill that which Gabriel had announced to her concerning the coming of Israel's Savior and Sovereign.[8]

Mary stayed with Elizabeth for about three months (v. 56), eventually coming home to face Joseph, her family, and the community. Her return took much faith and bravery because the threat of public disgrace—and even death—hung in the air. Pentecost again explains:

> Upon Mary's return from her visit in Judea, the fact of her pregnancy could not be veiled from Joseph, and Mary evidently communicated to him that she was pregnant. Since Joseph was a righteous man, it was inconceivable to him that he would marry one who was carrying what he would presume to be another man's child. The only explanation that came to his mind was that his betrothed had been unfaithful to him during her visit to her relatives and demonstrated that she was an immoral woman. Joseph had two options available to him. He could accuse her publicly of immorality and have her stoned (Deut. 22:13–21). Her death then would have broken the marriage contract. A second alternative was to divorce her. Because of Mary's pregnancy there was sufficient ground to seek an annulment of the marriage contract and to break the relationship existing between Joseph and Mary.[9]

Joseph, wanting to protect Mary and not "disgrace her, planned to send her away secretly" (Matt. 1:19). Although Joseph was a kind and gentle man who chose the least painful way to resolve the predicament, it's hard to imagine how the events prior to our Savior's birth could get any more tangled than they were at this point. What a mess!

The Miracle

In the middle of this big mess, however, God intervened once again—this time to perform a miracle.

8. J. Dwight Pentecost, *The Words and Works of Jesus Christ* (Grand Rapids, Mich.: Zondervan Publishing House, 1981), pp. 46–47.

9. Pentecost, *The Words and Works of Jesus Christ*, p. 54.

But when he [Joseph] considered this [divorcing Mary], behold, an angel of the Lord appeared to him in a dream, saying, "Joseph, son of David, do not be afraid to take Mary as your wife; for the Child who has been conceived in her is of the Holy Spirit. She will bear a Son; and you shall call His name Jesus, for He will save His people from their sins." (vv. 20–21)

That's all Joseph needed—he "did as the angel of the Lord commanded him, and took Mary as his wife, but kept her a virgin until she gave birth to a Son; and he called His name Jesus" (vv. 24–25).

Joseph obeyed and God performed a miracle—the birth of our Savior. God even arranged for the Baby to be born in Bethlehem, using a census Caesar Augustus wanted to take. Joseph, who just happened to be in David's line, had to return to David's city, Bethlehem, to register. Mary, as his betrothed, accompanied him and gave birth while they were there (Luke 2:1–7). So Jesus did indeed fulfill the prophecies regarding the Savior.

Without Jesus' perfect prophecy-fulfilling life and sacrificial death, our own lives would have no purpose, we would have no hope of a glorious future, and our deaths would only result in more death—eternal separation from God.

Alexander Fleming witnessed how one mess, a mere speck of dust, could save millions of lives. Joseph, on the other hand, witnessed how his mess would save the entire human race. Thank the Lord for godly messes!

 *Living Insights*

In the middle of her "mess," Mary praised the Lord in an exultation we call the Magnificat:

And Mary said:
"My soul exalts the Lord,
And my spirit has rejoiced in God my Savior.
For He has had regard for the humble state of His
    bondslave;
For behold, from this time on all generations will
    count me blessed.
For the Mighty One has done great things for me;
And holy is His name.
And His mercy is upon generation after generation

Toward those who fear Him.
He has done mighty deeds with His arm;
He has scattered those who were proud in the
thoughts of their heart.
He has brought down rulers from their thrones,
And exalted those who were humble.
He has filled the hungry with good things;
And sent away the rich empty-handed.
He has given help to Israel His servant,
In remembrance of His mercy,
As He spoke to our fathers,
To Abraham and his descendants forever."
(Luke 1:46–55)

Are you in a "mess" right now? Have you acted righteously, and yet it might appear as though you have done something wrong or foolish? Does it look like you might have to suffer punishment or some other negative consequence as a result?

Take a few moments to pray to the Lord. First, ask Him to bring an "Elizabeth" into your life—someone who can stand beside you, encourage you, and empower you to be strong and courageous. Also, pray that He will speak to others in the situation, as He did with Joseph. He probably won't appear to them in a dream, but He can move their hearts to treat you with compassion and understanding (see Gen 39:21; Neh. 1:11; Dan. 1:9). Finally, praise Him—praise Him because He shows mercy "toward those who fear Him." Praise Him now for His mercy to come.

Chapter 3

DEITY IN DIAPERS
Selected Scriptures

*C*hristmas. Let this simple, two-syllable word transport your mind from wherever you are to a dark, snowy evening on December 24. All of a sudden, you no longer see the desk or dirty clothes in front of you, and you no longer hear the low din of a busy office or home. Instead, you feel the warm embrace of a wool blanket as it cradles you in an overstuffed chair by a crackling fireplace. The curling steam from a mug of spiced cider nestled in your hands tickles your nose, while the slice of pumpkin pie on the coffee table tempts your eye.

Thoughts of Christmas certainly stimulate all five senses, stroking them with sights, sounds, smells, touches, and tastes of holiday seasons past. These memories, while enriching our own celebration of the Lord's birth, hold little resemblance to the first Christmas. W. Phillip Keller describes a much different scene in the stable:

> The sheep corral, filthy as only an Eastern animal enclosure can be, reeked pungently with manure and urine accumulated across the seasons. Joseph cleared a corner just large enough for Mary to lie down. Birth pains had started. She writhed in agony on the ground. . . .
>
> . . . Joseph swept away the dust and dirt from a small space in one of the hand-hewn mangers carved from the soft limestone rock. It was covered with cobwebs and debris fallen from the rock ceiling. . . .
>
> There, alone, unaided, without strangers or friends to witness her ordeal, in the darkness, Mary delivered her son. A more lowly or humble birth it is impossible to imagine. It was the unpretentious entrance, the stage entrance of the Son of man— the Son of God, God very God in human guise and form—upon earth's stage.
>
> In the dim darkness of the stable a new sound was heard. The infant cry of the newborn babe came clearly. For the first time deity was articulated directly

in sounds expressed through a human body.[1]

On that first, humble Christmas, our Lord Christ became a human being. In the first chapter, we focused on the preexistent and celestial nature of Jesus' deity. Now let's look at the other side of His nature—His humanity. Specifically, let's see how His earthly birth mixes with His divine nature to produce supernatural results.

The Miracles Surrounding Christ's Birth

Jesus' birth was every bit the human experience. Mary had just as much pain as any other woman, and the birth process was just as bloody and mysteriously beautiful. However, it was very different from any other birth before or since. It was surrounded by miracles—wonders that remain unmatched in their magnitude and importance for people of all times.

The Union of God and Man in One Body

Can a person be all God and all human at the same time? Let's take a look at two of the Gospel accounts to see what the Bible says. Among the Gospel writers, Luke especially emphasized Jesus' humanity and the earthly circumstances surrounding His birth:

> And she [Mary] gave birth to her firstborn son; and she wrapped Him in cloths, and laid Him in a manger, because there was no room for them in the inn. (Luke 2:7)

You can practically hear the baby cooing and see Mary nursing her child and rocking Him in her arms. The birth was indeed an earthly event—dirty diapers and all.

John's account, however, differs quite a bit from Luke's. John bypassed the earthly events of the Christmas story and emphasized instead Jesus' divine origin. Remember John's description from chapter one?

> In the beginning was the Word, and the Word was with God, and the Word was God. (John 1:1)

No stories of Bethlehem. No images of babies in swaddling clothes or lying in mangers. No genealogy of the Savior. After all, God has

---

1. W. Phillip Keller, *Rabboni* (Old Tappan, N.J.: Fleming H. Revell Co., 1977), pp. 56–57.

no forefathers. Nor did John give any details about Jesus' birth and childhood. His was the last Gospel written so he didn't need or want to reiterate what Matthew and Luke had already communicated so well. Also, while these aspects of Jesus' life are important, they didn't contribute to John's purpose in writing his Gospel.

Taking these different accounts together, though, we can formulate an understanding of one of the greatest miracles of all time—that God and man coexisted in the same body at the same time. Theologians refer to Jesus as the "theanthropic person." This strange term comes from the Greek words *theos,* which means "God," and *anthropos,* which means "man." Jesus, then, was the "God-man person." Truly a miracle!

The theanthropic nature of Jesus is important to us because it establishes His authority to come as the Savior of the world, to conquer sin and death, and to offer us everlasting life.

The Virgin Birth

One of the most important pieces of biblical evidence for Jesus' theanthropic nature is the Virgin Birth. Luke points out Mary's virginity in his description of Gabriel's announcement:

> Now in the sixth month the angel Gabriel was sent from God to a city in Galilee called Nazareth, to a *virgin* engaged to a man whose name was Joseph, of the descendants of David; and the virgin's name was Mary. (Luke 1:26–27, emphasis added)

Luke, however, was not the only Gospel writer to make this point. Matthew also mentions it:

> Now the birth of Jesus Christ was as follows: when His mother Mary had been betrothed to Joseph, *before they came together* [sexually] she was found to be with child by the Holy Spirit. (Matt. 1:18, emphasis added)

The Virgin Birth is essential to Jesus being both God and man. It's the key to Christ's identity and the significance of His theanthropic nature. Biblical scholar John M. Frame says that if Jesus

> were born of two human parents, it is very difficult to conceive how he could have been exempted from the guilt of Adam's sin and become a new head to the

human race. . . . Yet Jesus' sinlessness as the new head of the human race and as the atoning lamb of God is absolutely vital to our salvation (2 Cor. 5:21; 1 Pet. 2:22–24; Heb. 4:15; 7:26; Rom. 5:18–19).

. . . The birth of Christ, in which the initiative and power are all of God, is an apt picture of God's saving grace. . . . It teaches us that salvation is by God's act, not our human effort. The birth of Jesus is like our new birth, which is also by the Holy Spirit; it is a new creation (II Cor. 5:17).[2]

The Virgin Birth remains a cornerstone of Christian belief. It influences what we think and affirm about Jesus' true identity.

He Emptied Himself

From our human viewpoint, Jesus' coming was filled with miracles and mystery. From His perspective, however, it must have looked and felt quite different. It's hard for us to imagine what He gave up by becoming a man. He went from sitting at the right hand of God to lying in a feeding trough, from ruling the universe to becoming an object of scorn. Despite all this, He displayed a servant's heart. Paul offered these words about Jesus' incarnation:

Although He existed in the form of God, did not regard equality with God a thing to be grasped, but emptied Himself, taking the form of a bond-servant, and being made in the likeness of men. Being found in appearance as a man, He humbled Himself by becoming obedient to the point of death, even death on a cross. (Phil. 2:6–8)

Jesus, by not regarding "equality with God a thing to be grasped," emptied Himself of His divine glory and privileges. He didn't think so highly of Himself that He had to cling to the advantages of His position. Instead, He set aside the privileges of deity to take on the lot of a slave. It must have been an incredibly humbling experience to live His selfless, obedient life and then die His selfless, obedient death.

---

2. John M. Frame, "Virgin Birth of Jesus," in *Evangelical Dictionary of Theology*, ed. Walter A. Elwell (Grand Rapids, Mich.: Baker Book House, 1984), p. 1145. See also Millard J. Erickson, *Introducing Christian Doctrine*, ed. L. Arnold Hustad (Grand Rapids, Mich.: Baker Book House, 1992), p. 221.

Remembering the Miraculous in Christmas

Jesus underwent the painful process of emptying Himself for a very important reason—to offer us eternal life. Without His life and ultimate sacrifice of dying on the cross, we would have been destined to live eternally without Him. As Paul put it in 2 Corinthians 8:9,

> For you know the grace of our Lord Jesus Christ, that though He was rich, yet for your sake He became poor, so that you through His poverty might become rich.

The first Christmas was quite different from what we experience today. But it can still hold some of its miraculous and mysterious nature if we choose to remember that the baby Jesus was more than a mere baby. He was deity in diapers. He was and is the greatest gift of all.

Living Insights

Up in the attic, in the far corner, lay all the boxes of tangled lights, ornaments, and Christmas crafts. One of the most treasured crates among them is the one containing the Nativity scene. The kids don't get to unpack this one—only Mom or Dad can handle its contents. Carefully, gently, the delicate porcelain figures are unrolled from their newsprint wrappers and placed artfully on a mantle or shelf. The shepherds, angels, animals, magi, Joseph, and Mary all stand oblivious to the songs and holiday din around them. Rather, they stand in a state of perpetual awe of the baby Jesus.

Take the next few minutes to step into that Nativity scene. Close your eyes and imagine yourself there. What would you say to Jesus to thank Him for His miraculous and sacrificial appearance as a man? What would you do to honor His generous act? Write out your response.

_____

_____

_____

_____

_____

_____

_____

_____

_____

_____

Now that you've thought through what you'd say to Him, why don't you go ahead and say it? Bow your head and thank Him and praise Him for what He's done.

Chapter 4

RESPONDING TO THE REDEEMER

Selected Scriptures

C hristianity, in its purest form," writes Max Lucado, "is nothing more than seeing Jesus. Christian service, in its purest form, is nothing more than imitating him who we see. To see His Majesty and to imitate him, that is the sum of Christianity."[1] Truly seeing Jesus for who He is the basic starting point of the Christian life, but that vision compels us to do more than merely stand and look, as if Jesus were just a marvelous work of art. It draws us irresistibly to a place where we feel the need to *respond* to who we see—in faith certainly, and also in truth to where we are in life.

Some of us are new believers reveling in the fresh joy of God's saving love. Others of us gamely follow Christ with a childlike trust wherever He may lead. Still others of us hold a more tentative faith; we love the Lord but can't figure life out and strain to understand God's plan in it all.

The way we respond to Jesus, then, hinges on how much we understand about what He's done for us, how much we grasp His plans for the future, how much we've been hurt by life, and so many other factors. There is no one right way for Christians to respond to their Savior but as many ways as there are people.

The Gospels certainly bear this out. Let's spend some time looking at a variety of people and their variety of responses to Jesus. Some we know were fellow believers; some, like the Magi, we're not sure of. All of their responses, though, can open up new ways for us to interact with God's own majestic Son.

Scenes from Scripture

The Gospels overflow with examples of people responding to Jesus. Some groups, like the Pharisees, hated Him. Others, especially the poor and sick, flocked to Him with hope and affection. But we can probably learn the most from the more intimate responses He

---

1. Max Lucado, *God Came Near* (Portland, Ore.: Multnomah Press, 1987), p. 6.

received. So let's step away from the crowds and cliques and watch those who saw Him up close.

The Shepherds in the Fields

"The birth of Christ," observes Matthew Henry, "was notified to the Jewish shepherds by an angel, to the Gentile philosophers by a star: to both God spoke in their own language, and in the way they were best acquainted with."[2] Listen to what the angel had to say:

> In the same region there were some shepherds staying out in the fields and keeping watch over their flock by night. And an angel of the Lord suddenly stood before them, and the glory of the Lord shone around them; and they were terribly frightened. But the angel said to them, "Do not be afraid; for behold, I bring you good news of great joy which will be for all the people; for today in the city of David there has been born for you a Savior, who is Christ the Lord. This will be a sign for you: you will find a baby wrapped in cloths and lying in a manger." And suddenly there appeared with the angel a multitude of the heavenly host praising God and saying,
> "Glory to God in the highest,
> And on earth peace among men with whom He
> is pleased." (Luke 2:8–14)

Wow! What a way to break the monotony of watching sheep through the night!

Do you ever wonder why God chose to announce His Son's birth to shepherds? *The International Standard Bible Encyclopedia* tells us that "shepherding was serious, demanding, and strenuous work. Nevertheless, the true or faithful shepherd was thought to have a disposition that was altogether admirable: thoughtful, tender, gentle, strong, resourceful in times of danger."[3] Not to mention vigilant.

---

2. Matthew Henry, *Commentary on the Whole Bible*, one-vol. ed. (Grand Rapids, Mich.: Zondervan Publishing House, Regency Reference Library, 1960), p. 1206. Angels were intimately intertwined with Jewish history (see Gen. 16:7–11; 21:17; 22:11–15; 28:12; 31:11; 32:1; Exod. 14:19; 23:20, 23; 32:34; Num. 22; Josh. 5:13–15; Judg. 13; 1 Kings 19; Ps. 34:7; 35:5–6; 78:25, 49; 91:11; 103:20; 148:2; Dan. 6:22; 7:16; 8:15–19; 9:21–23; 10:5–21; Zech. 1:9–19; 2:3; 4:1; 5:5–10; 6:4–5).

3. Paul Leslie Garber, "Sheep; Shepherd," in *The International Standard Bible Encyclopedia*, rev. ed., gen. ed. Geoffrey W. Bromiley (Grand Rapids, Mich.: William B. Eerdmans Publishing Co., 1988), vol. 4, p. 464.

Fighting off fatigue and pain, good shepherds were ever-watchful over their precious charges, protecting the sheep from other animals, thieves, bad weather, disease, and their own tendency to wander off. What better eyes than the watchful eyes of shepherds to witness the arrival of God's own precious Lamb?

After the angels returned to heaven, the amazed shepherds must have trusted God to take care of their sheep because they decided to "go straight to Bethlehem" to see what the Lord had done (v. 15).

> So they came in a hurry and found their way to Mary and Joseph, and the baby as He lay in the manger. When they had seen this, they made known the statement which had been told them about this Child. And all who heard it wondered at the things which were told them by the shepherds. . . . The shepherds went back, glorifying and praising God for all that they had heard and seen, just as had been told them. (vv. 16–18, 20)

Did you follow the shepherds' response? They heard the Good News, sought immediately to see what God had done, told others what the angel had told them, and glorified and praised the Lord! The coming of their Savior was a time for joy—and evangelism too. Commentator Norval Geldenhuys explains.

> Just as these simple shepherds are the first persons to whom the glad tidings concerning the birth of Christ are communicated, so in turn they are the first proclaimers of the event to others. It is probable that their flock was intended for offerings in the temple, as flocks for this purpose were kept in the vicinity of Bethlehem. . . . In this case they would ere long have gone to Jerusalem and would there also have told the whole story to the pious people who were awaiting the coming of the promised Messiah. In this manner they would have prepared persons like Simeon and Anna (verses 25–40) for their welcoming of the Christ-child.[4]

4. Norval Geldenhuys, *Commentary on the Gospel of Luke*, The New International Commentary on the New Testament series (Grand Rapids, Mich.: William B. Eerdmans Publishing Co., 1979), pp. 113–14.

So theirs is an example of exuberant, responsive faith that drops everything and comes running to see and share the wonders God has performed. Mary's response, though, is a little different.

Mary

While the shepherds rejoiced, Mary quietly watched, listened, and soaked it all in.

> But Mary treasured all these things, pondering them
> in her heart. (v. 19)

The word *treasured* in Greek, *suntereo*, means "to keep in the memory";[5] and its companion in the next phrase, *pondering* (*sumballo* in Greek), means "to throw together, hence to discuss, consider, meet with." In other words, Mary tried to put together a whole picture out of the many pieces of the Messiah puzzle God had given her so far. She mulled over "the inbreaking of God in her life."[6] Everything from Gabriel's first announcement to Joseph's dream to Elizabeth's reaction and now to the shepherds' angelic revelation were part of her musings, reinforcing for her the divinity of her Son. But did she fully understand what all of this meant? Geldenhuys asks,

> Was Mary, then, a perfect being who immediately, perfectly and permanently grasped the full significance of the angels' tidings, the supernatural conception, and so forth? Would she not, as a fallible mortal, also sometimes through the years (as was likewise the case with John the Baptist) have times of doubt and uncertainty?[7]

Of course. She needed time to understand and grow in her faith in God's Son. As William Hendriksen notes,

> Her prayerful "putting together" of the things she had experienced, seen, and heard, was blessed by God and in course of time produced the result he had

---

5. Gerhard Kittel and Gerhard Friedrich, eds., *Theological Dictionary of the New Testament*, translated and abridged in one volume by Geoffrey W. Bromiley (1985; reprint, Grand Rapids, Mich.: William B. Eerdmans Publishing Co., 1992), p. 1176.

6. Darrell L. Bock, *Luke*, The IVP New Testament Commentary Series (Downers Grove, Ill.: InterVarsity Press, 1994), p. 56.

7. Geldenhuys, *Commentary on the Gospel of Luke*, p. 114.

determined from eternity. To be sure, on Mary's part there were missteps along the way, but the end was victory.[8]

The Magi

From joyful evangelism to quiet pondering, we now see a third response from the Magi when they found Jesus.

> Now after Jesus was born in Bethlehem of Judea in the days of Herod the king, magi from the east arrived in Jerusalem, saying, "Where is He who has been born King of the Jews? For we saw His star in the east and have come to worship Him." . . . The star, which they had seen in the east, went on before them until it came and stood over the place where the child was. When they saw the star, they rejoiced exceedingly with great joy. After coming into the house they saw the Child with Mary His mother; and they fell to the ground and worshiped Him. Then, opening their treasures, they presented to Him gifts of gold, frankincense, and myrrh. (Matt. 2:1–2, 9b–11)

To the stargazers God sent a star, and like the shepherds, the Magi followed where God led. Their statement about "His star" in verse 2 "strongly suggests that they have studied the Scriptures as well as the heavens. Was not a star to herald Israel's king, and were not the Gentiles to come to his light to pay him homage (Num. 24:17–18; Isa. 60:3)?"[9] Quite possibly, these Magi may have come from Babylon, "where a sizable Jewish settlement wielded considerable influence,"[10] and from whom they may have learned the Hebrew Scriptures.

---

8. William Hendriksen, *Exposition of the Gospel According to Luke*, New Testament Commentary series (Grand Rapids, Mich.: Baker Book House, 1978), p. 158. When twelve-year-old Jesus remained in Jerusalem after the Passover, Mary and Joseph found Him in the temple after a three-day search. There He "amazed" the rabbis with His insight and puzzled His mother with His knowledge of His calling: "Why is it that you were looking for Me? Did you not know that I had to be in My Father's house?" Though she did not understand His meaning, she again "treasured all these things in her heart" (Luke 2:41–51).

9. J. Knox Chamblin, "Matthew," in the *Evangelical Commentary on the Bible*, ed. Walter A. Elwell (Grand Rapids, Mich.: Baker Book House, 1989), p. 726.

10. D. A. Carson, "Matthew," in *The Expositor's Bible Commentary*, gen. ed. Frank E. Gaebelein (Grand Rapids, Mich.: Zondervan Publishing House, Regency Reference Library, 1984), vol. 8, p. 85, see also p. 86.

What was their response to the King of the Jews? Worship—joyful, reverent, generous worship. The Greek word for *worship*, *proskuneō*, is used in the New Testament "only in relation to a divine object."[11] So Matthew indicated that they were doing more than merely paying homage to an earthly king. Their worship was "truly offered to the Ruler of the world."[12]

Where God's chosen people—Jesus' own people—responded with apathy and antipathy (Matt. 2:3–8, 12–23), Matthew shows us that the Gentiles gave the appropriate response.

The Disciples

The disciples provide us with still another response. Let's look at Jesus' first interactions with Peter, Andrew, James, John, and Matthew (Levi).

> As He was going along by the Sea of Galilee, He saw Simon and Andrew, the brother of Simon, casting a net in the sea; for they were fishermen. And Jesus said to them, "Follow Me, and I will make you become fishers of men." Immediately they left their nets and followed Him. Going on a little farther, He saw James the son of Zebedee, and John his brother, who were also in the boat mending the nets. Immediately He called them; and they left their father Zebedee in the boat with the hired servants, and went away to follow Him. . . .
>
> . . . As He passed by, He saw Levi the son of Alphaeus sitting in the tax booth, and He said to him, "Follow Me!" And he got up and followed Him. (Mark 1:16–20; 2:14)

"Immediately" they "followed." Let's remember what these men gave up by answering Christ's call: they walked away from their livelihoods to follow Jesus, a Man who gave them no promise of financial security. Yet they trusted Him to provide for their needs as well as their families' needs, displaying an openness to step out in

---

11. Kittel and Friedrich, eds., abridged by Bromiley, *Theological Dictionary of the New Testament*, p. 949.

12. Gerhard Friedrich, ed., *Theological Dictionary of the New Testament*, trans. and ed. Geoffrey W. Bromiley (1968; reprint, Grand Rapids, Mich.: William B. Eerdmans Publishing Co., 1993), vol. 6, p. 764.

faith and follow Christ wherever He would lead—without hesitation. They would be His "fishers of men," drawing others to the same Christ whom they were drawn to themselves (see Matt. 28:18–20).

Spotlight on You

How do you respond to Christ? Are you, like the shepherds, eager to spread the Good News (see Matt. 28:18–20)? Do you, like Mary, ponder the things God has revealed about His Son (see Heb. 12:2–3)? Like the Magi, do you worship the King—and maybe more, do you yearn for His righteous reign (see Ps. 72; Phil. 2:10–11; Rev. 5:6–14; 19:11–16)? Are you, like the disciples, willing to obediently follow Christ without hesitation (see Matt. 11:29; 16:24; 1 Pet. 2:21)?

For us Christians, all of these responses have a place in our lives. Do they for you? What are your eyes focused on in life? Do you keep Jesus in plain sight, or does He end up on the periphery more than you would like? It's hard to respond to someone whom we've lost sight of, isn't it? Max Lucado writes,

> Mark it down. We are what we see. If we see only ourselves, our tombstones will have the same epitaph Paul used to describe enemies of Christ: "Their God is their own appetite, they glory in their shame, and this world is the limit of their horizon" [Phil. 3:19 PHILLIPS]. Humans were never meant to dwell in the stale fog of the lowlands with no vision of their Creator.
>
> That's why God came near. To be seen. . . .
>
> Only in seeing his Maker does a man truly become man. For in seeing his Creator man catches a glimpse of what he was intended to be. He who would see his God would then see the reason for death and the purpose of time. Destiny? Tomorrow? Truth? All are questions within the reach of the man who knows his source.
>
> It is in seeing Jesus that man sees his Source.[13]

We haven't personally seen the glory of angels in the night sky, the Baby Jesus in the manger, the Infant on His mother's lap, or

---

13. Lucado, *God Came Near*, pp. 79, 46.

the Man teaching and healing and calming storms and dying at the center of the worst storm ever. But with our spiritual eyes, we have seen Him in the word pictures He has preserved in the Bible, haven't we? And it is with these eyes of faith that He would have us see what we should become—"conformed to the image of His Son" and transformed to "prove what the will of God is, that which is good and acceptable and perfect" (Rom. 8:29; 12:2).

There is no greater calling, no greater "shaper" of our lives than how we respond to Jesus, the majestic Son of God.

Living Insights

Do you have a clear sense of your calling? Do you wonder where you fit within God's great scheme of things? Many of us understand that our faith defines our life—our beliefs determine our life's contour through the choices we make. Within this larger calling of reflecting Christ to the world, though, is a more specific calling that a lot of us struggle with. Why? Because we're not sure what God has called us to be. We don't exactly know what our unique purpose is as individuals.

One prominent businessman admitted,

> "As you know, I have been very fortunate in my career and I've made a lot of money—far more than I ever dreamed of, far more than I could ever spend, far more than my family needs. . . .
>
> "To be honest, one of my motives for making so much money was simple—to have the money to hire people to do what I don't like doing. But there's one thing I've never been able to hire anyone to do for me: find my own sense of purpose and fulfillment. I'd give anything to discover that." [14]

If you feel like that businessman, take heart. God wants you to know how you contribute to the Body of Christ, and He has given you a number of clues to discover your calling for yourself.

1. *Your spiritual gifts.* Do you have a knack for teaching, administrating, giving, showing mercy, extending hospitality, sharing the

14. Quoted by Os Guinness in *The Call: Finding and Fulfilling the Central Purpose of Your Life* (Nashville, Tenn.: Word Publishing, 1998), p. 1.

Gospel? God has given you a specific combination of gifts with which to accomplish your call (see 1 Cor. 12; 14; Rom. 12). What are your spiritual gifts?

_____

_____

_____

_____

2. *Your natural talents.* Are you good at singing, carpentry, writing, painting, dancing, speaking, dealing with people, coaching, cooking, or computer work? God wants to use the talents He has given you. To what are you drawn that you do well?

_____

_____

_____

_____

3. *Your areas of interest.* God has given you passions for certain things. What do you enjoy or feel strongly about that you can use for His glory?

_____

_____

_____

_____

4. *Your personality type.* Your personality determines how you'll use your gifts, talents, and interests. Do you tend to be introverted or extroverted? People-oriented or task-oriented? Warm or reserved? Gentle or brusque? Funny or serious? Do you like to work alone or with people? Be in the spotlight or behind the scenes?

_____

_____

_____

5. *Your leadership style.* Visionaries like to break new ground—"go where no one has gone before!" Managers, on the other hand, like to make existing systems run better. Which style do you lean toward?

_____

_____

_____

_____

As you can see, finding your specific calling will take prayer and some deep probing in a lot of different areas. God has crafted you into a unique and intricate person to serve the needs of His kingdom and reflect a facet of Christ that only you can show. So keep your eyes trained on your Savior, that you may become like the One you see in everything you do.

Chapter 5

LIFE . . . AS GOD INTENDED IT
Selected Scriptures

H ave you ever heard of the anchorites? Renegades of the third century, they sold all their possessions, fled to the deserts of Egypt, and lived as destitute hermits. Were they political revolutionaries? Fugitives from justice? Actually, they were the first monks.

The first anchorite, Saint Anthony, remains the most famous of these ascetics.[1] In his efforts to defeat the temptations of Satan and live a pure life for Christ, Anthony went to extremes.

> He kept a vigil to such an extent that he often continued the whole night without sleep; and this not once but often, to the marvel of others. He ate once a day, after sunset, sometimes once in two days, and often even in four. His food was bread and salt, his drink, water only. . . . A rush mat served him to sleep upon, but for the most part he lay upon the bare ground.[2]

At one point, Anthony "went to live in a tomb in an abandoned cemetery."[3] Some anchorites even made themselves "eunuchs for the Kingdom."[4] Ouch!

Is this the way God wants us to live—isolating and inflicting pain on ourselves to make sure we don't become too enamored with earthly life? Is this what Jesus taught? What *did* He have to say about life, anyway?

The apostle John tells us what He said:

> "I came that they may have life, and have it abundantly." (John 10:10b)

---

1. Historians cannot decisively determine if Anthony was indeed the very first anchorite. Some sources suggest that a man named Paul (not the apostle) may have been the first. The bulk of tradition, however, points to Anthony.

2. Athanasius, *The Life of Antony,* in *Readings in the History of Christian Theology,* comp. William C. Placher (Philadelphia, Pa.: Westminster Press, 1988), vol. 1, p. 130.

3. Justo L. González, *The Story of Christianity* (San Francisco, Calif.: HarperSanFrancisco, 1984), vol. 1, p. 140.

4. González, *The Story of Christianity,* vol. 1, p. 137.

Life as God intended it is abundant. But what exactly does this mean? Let's gather some clues from John's Gospel, where we'll see that the abundant life is inextricably tied to the abundant love of God's Son.

A Clue to Life in John's Gospel

"Life," as Leon Morris tells us, "is one of John's characteristic concepts: he uses the word 36 times, whereas no other New Testament writing has it more than 17 times ([in] Revelation; next come Romans with 14 times and 1 John with 13 times)."[5] Remember, John also wrote Revelation and 1 John, which means he taught on this concept at least sixty-six times!

Why would he spend so much time on this idea? Because the Spirit revealed to him that true life and knowing the Lord are the same thing. John remembered Jesus praying before His disciples, "This is eternal life, that they may know You, the only true God, and Jesus Christ whom You have sent" (John 17:3). When John wrote about life, he linked it seventeen times with the word *eternal*—a word that undoubtedly refers "more to the kind of life than its duration. It is the life of God shared with His people, therefore both imperishable and blessed."[6]

Eternal life, then, is our future hope as well as our present reality; because when we put our faith in Christ, eternal life begins for us (John 5:24). We won't know its full glory until heaven, where we'll be with the Lord and delivered completely from sin at last. But we surely have a taste of it now, and that sweet savor keeps us hungering for more.

Jesus, the Giver of Life

Who gives us life abundantly? Jesus Christ Himself. As John testifies:

> In Him was life, and the life was the Light of men.
> (John 1:4)

5. Leon Morris, The Gospel according to John, rev. ed., The New International Commentary on the New Testament (Grand Rapids, Mich.: William B. Eerdmans Publishing Co., 1995), p. 73.

6. Everett F. Harrison, "Life," in The International Standard Bible Encyclopedia, gen. ed. Geoffrey W. Bromiley (1986; reprint, Grand Rapids, Mich.: William B. Eerdmans Publishing Co., 1987), vol. 3, p. 132.

"For just as the Father raises the dead and gives them life, even so the Son also gives life to whom He wishes." (5:21)

Jesus said to them, "I am the bread of life; he who comes to Me will not hunger, and he who believes in Me will never thirst." (6:35)

Then Jesus again spoke to them, saying, "I am the Light of the world; he who follows Me will not walk in the darkness, but will have the Light of life." (8:12)

Jesus said to her, "I am the resurrection and the life; he who believes in Me will live even if he dies." (11:25)

Jesus said to him, "I am the way, and the truth, and the life; no one comes to the Father but through Me." (14:6)

These have been written so that you may believe that Jesus is the Christ, the Son of God; and that believing you may have life in His name. (20:31)

Through His grace, Jesus bestows life on us—and bestows it plentifully. That's what the Greek word for *abundantly* in John 10:10 means: *perissos*, "superabundant."[7] In that passage, the relationship between Jesus, the Good Shepherd, and His sheep "is marked by the desire and pleasure of the shepherd to give his sheep not just enough but plenty—a characteristic repeatedly mentioned elsewhere (e.g., Psalm 23, Ezekiel 34)."[8] Did you catch that? It's Jesus' *desire and pleasure* to lavish His loving care on His sheep, to give us life abundantly.

Let's look at this life He has given us to see what it is . . . and what it isn't.

---

7. Gerhard Kittel and Gerhard Friedrich, *Theological Dictionary of the New Testament*, translated and abridged in one volume by Geoffrey W. Bromiley (1985; reprint, Grand Rapids, Mich.: William B. Eerdmans Publishing Co., 1992), p. 828.

8. Herman N. Ridderbos, *The Gospel according to John: A Theological Commentary*, trans. John Vriend (Grand Rapids, Mich.: William B. Eerdmans Publishing Co., 1997), p. 359.

What the Abundant Life Is . . . and Isn't

Sometimes the best way to get a grasp on something is to compare it with what it is not. So let's sketch out some facts about the nature of the abundant life, determine what it isn't, and fill in the blanks from there.

What It Is

The abundant life is . . .

- *Eternal:* Because Christ is eternal (John 1:1–2), and He is the life who has conquered death (14:6; 10:17; 11:25), the life He gives us is everlasting (3:15–16).

- *God-made:* Jesus is the One who brought everything into being (1:3) and made us God's children (vv. 12–13). He has taken the initiative toward us, and we have done nothing to contribute to this gift of eternal, abundant life (4:10).

- *Spiritual:* The abundant life is spiritual, not natural. It isn't something we're born with; it comes when we're born again (3:3, 5–6; 4:23–24). The life Jesus gives is an eternal dimension of living that is untainted by the sin of our human nature.

- *In Christ:* As we saw in the verses from John, new life comes only through Christ. John reiterated the thoughts from his Gospel in his first letter: "God has given us eternal life, and this life is in His Son. He who has the Son has the life; he who does not have the Son of God does not have the life" (1 John 5:11–12).

What It Isn't

Luke's Gospel sheds some light on what the abundant life is not:

> Then He said to them, "Beware, and be on your guard against every form of greed; for not even when one has an abundance does his life consist of his possessions." (Luke 12:15)

So the abundant life is not measured by

- possessions
- income
- health
- status

35

The so-called "health and wealth gospel" is really no gospel at all. It appeals to our human craving for comfort and starves us for the sustenance only Christ can give.

So What Does the Abundant Life Look Like?

The abundant life is "the life for which we were created."[9] When we have abundant life, we live in the light of the eternal life that has already begun in us through faith in Christ. We live out and live by heaven's values—the values of a world restored to perfection. In this world God "will wipe away every tear from their eyes; there will no longer be any death; there will no longer be any mourning, crying, or pain; the first things have passed away" (Rev. 21:4). What do these values look like? Paul listed some in Galatians 5:

> The fruit of the Spirit is love, joy, peace, patience, kindness, goodness, faithfulness, gentleness, self-control; against such things there is no law. (vv. 22–23)

Peter adds more in 2 Peter 1:

> Applying all diligence, in your faith supply moral excellence, and in your moral excellence, knowledge, and in your knowledge, self-control, and in your self-control, perseverance, and in your perseverance, godliness, and in your godliness, brotherly kindness, and in your brotherly kindness, love. (vv. 5–7)

To live abundantly is to be ever aware of the grace God has lavished on us (Eph. 1:3–8a). It is to be rooted and grounded in the love He has showered on us (3:17–20). It is to be anchored in the certain hope of Christ's coming again and His consummation of all His plans (Rom. 15:13). To live abundantly is to make choices that reflect the reality of Christ and His kingdom—to shape our present in light of our future. A. J. Conyers explains,

> How we respond to this moment—this poor man in our midst, this starving child in our community, this prisoner in our institutions, the very humblest and meanest of those who enter our lives today—is in fact the way we greet the last moment of life, the

---

9. Bruce Milne, *The Message of John: Here Is Your King!* The Bible Speaks Today series (Downers Grove, Ill.: InterVarsity Press, 1993), p. 148.

last moment of the planet Earth, the first moment of a newly manifest and apparent kingdom of God.[10]

It's not an easy life, but it's the real life . . . and it's the best life there could be.

Learning to Live Abundantly

What are some ways we can start living the abundant life today? The first and only place to start is by placing our faith in Jesus Christ. Just knowing about Him and what He has said and done won't do. The Bible says that even the demons know that Jesus is God and fear Him (James 2:19). This kind of mental assent won't bring us life. Instead, we must trust in Him, decide to place our faith in His life and death and resurrection, so His blood can supply the abundant life we lost at the Fall. When we trust Christ in this way, we get Him inside our hearts where He can do some good.

With this faith in Jesus Christ, we have at least four ways of living the abundant life.

- *Soar.* Live above the drag of fear, superstition, worry, and negativism by taking our needs to God.

- *Ignore.* Refuse to take our cues from those who operate from only the human perspective by listening to God's voice instead of the general public's.

- *Risk.* Break out of our comfort zones by trusting God to know more than we do.

- *Release.* Let go of our craving for control by allowing Christ to be in the driver's seat.

God never wanted us to run away from the world, to try to escape it like some of the anchorites sought to do. Instead, He wants us to engage our world—to be in it but not of it. And the only way we can fulfill His desire is to enter into the abundant life He offers.

Have you trusted Christ as your Savior? If you haven't, that's the first place to begin. Pray now, won't you? (Please refer to the prayer at the end of chapter 1.) God has loved you from the beginning of time and eagerly waits to call you His child and lavish His love on you.

10. A. J. Conyers, *The End: What Jesus Really Said about the Last Things* (Downers Grove, Ill.: InterVarsity Press, 1995), p. 53.

If Christ is already your Savior, are you taking part in the abundant life He offers? If not, why not? Could it be that you are trying to live a "Christian life" without much of Christ in it? If that's the case, don't lose hope. In our next chapter, we'll learn how to have an abiding relationship with the Savior we already trust.

Living Insights

David wrote in Psalm 16:

> You will make known to me the path of life;
> In Your presence is fullness of joy;
> In Your right hand there are pleasures forever. (v. 11)

And God has made known who the Path of Life is, hasn't He?

> Jesus said to him, "I am the way, and the truth, and the life." (John 14:6a)

When you think of living for Christ, are joy and pleasure the first things that come to mind? Or are you more in sync with the spirit of the anchorites—making your way as hard and painful as possible to always suffer with Christ? Oh, you may not camp out in a cemetery or starve yourself, but sometimes we create rules and regulations, do's and don'ts, that really stifle Christ's life rather than foster it. What has been your experience?

_____

_____

_____

What has been your picture of God? Are you sure He wants to lavish His grace and love on you? Or do you think of Him as angry, waiting to wallop you whenever you mess up?

_____

_____

_____

Paul tells us in Colossians that Jesus "is the image of the invisible God" and "in Him all the fullness of Deity dwells in bodily form" (Col. 1:15a; 2:9). Jesus Himself said, "He who has seen Me has seen the Father" (John 14:9). If your life is more parched than plentiful regarding God's grace, spend some time learning to see God more clearly in the mirror of Christ. Linger over some images from John's Gospel that show the abundant grace, love, and life that Jesus offers, jotting down your reflections in the space provided.

John 1:14–18 _____

_____

_____

3:15–16 _____

_____

_____

4:13–14 _____

_____

_____

5:24 _____

_____

_____

6:37–40 _____

_____

_____

8:1–11 _____

_____

_____

8:31–32 _____

_____

9:1–7 _____

_____

_____

10:7–18, 27–28 _____

_____

_____

11:17–44 _____

_____

_____

12:44–47 _____

_____

_____

13:1–15 _____

_____

_____

Chapter 6

ABIDING IN CHRIST

John 15:1–11

As we saw in our last chapter, we can't live an abundant life apart from Christ. Sometimes, though, in spite of the fact that we've been born again by faith in Jesus, we tend to want to grow by ourselves. Like an infant who yells, "Let me do it!" we sometimes want to "do" the Christian life our way.

This, of course, gets us off the path of life and leads us to the dead end of our desires. We're still saved, but we certainly aren't partaking of the joy and pleasure of our new life.

The secret to remaining in a life abounding with God's grace is to remain with Christ, or as He put it, to "abide in" Him. Let's join Jesus in the Upper Room as He explains to His disciples what it means to stay rooted in Him.

Setting the Scene

The Last Supper has been eaten, the dishes cleared from the table. Flickering lamps splash the shadows of twelve men on the walls of an upper room in Jerusalem. Earlier there were thirteen. But one has slipped into the night to keep a dark appointment, where he will sell the Savior for thirty pieces of silver.

Jesus knows that time is short. These final moments before His arrest are crucial. The lessons must stick; the images must last. That's why He has eaten the Passover meal with His disciples, depicting His sacrificial death (John 13). He has imparted humility by washing their feet and has comforted them with heaven and the promise of the coming Helper (chap. 14). Now He must remind them that the spiritual life can be lived only in connection with the spiritual life-giver—Jesus Himself, the Vine.

Overall Survey of John 15

Jesus' words in John 15 center on relationships, as the overview chart on the following page shows.

By describing Himself as the Vine (vv. 1–11), Jesus makes it clear that our relationship with Him should be the most important and the most intimate. From that foundation we build loving

41

SURVEY CHART OF JOHN 15

For centuries, the fifteenth chapter of John has been a source of encouragement and inspiration for God's people. While it is written in simple terms, it contains some of the most profound, valuable, and helpful truths Jesus ever taught. Here is a chart that provides an overall survey of how the chapter fits together.

Suggested Theme of John 15: *The Most Important Relationships a Believer Maintains*

Overall Survey of Chapter

SECTION	RELATIONSHIP	KEY TERM	EMPHASIS
Verses 1–11	Believer with Christ	"Abide" (10 times in 11 verses)	Union
Verses 12–17	Believer with Believer	"Love" (4 times in 6 verses)	Communion
Verses 18–27	Believer with the World	"Hate" (8 times in 10 verses)	Disunion

relationships with other believers, having communion with those who share the same Spirit (vv. 12–17). We don't have this common bond with the world, which will often react violently to the Light we live by (vv. 18–27).

We're often distracted by the taunts and attacks of our enemies and by our involvements with other believers. But Christ alone is our center and our reason for being, and our life with Him must come before anything else. With that in mind, let's turn to verses 1–11.

Specific Study of the Vine and the Branches

There's plenty of truth to be harvested here. Let's begin by making four observations. These are solid stakes around which the rest of the passage grows.

Four Important Observations

First, *the instruction is for believers only.* Jesus addresses those already connected to the Vine. Rather than urging non-Christians to become Christians, His words encourage Christians to keep growing.

Second, *these verses revolve around a single symbol—the Vine and His branches.* The language of the vineyard would have been easily understood by Jesus' eleven disciples. Not only was the society in which they lived primarily agricultural, but they were Jews, which means they would have been familiar with God's use of vine imagery to describe Israel (see Ps. 80:8–16; Isa. 5:1–7).

Third, *the main subject is abiding.* Throughout the passage, Jesus repeatedly tells us to *abide* in Him. *Abide* is a term of close connection and dependence. In the Greek, it literally means "remain, stay." [1]

Fourth, *abiding results in fruit-bearing.* Jesus wants the world to recognize us as His own by the way we live. So the stronger our connection to the Vine, the more fruit we will bear. *Fruit* is a display of Christlike qualities in the life of a believer (see Gal. 5:22–23).

Key Interpretations

Now let's get into the thick of the passage and analyze the three main symbols—the vine, the vinedresser, and the branches.

The *vine,* of course, represents Jesus Christ (v. 1). He is *the*

1. Walter Bauer, *A Greek-English Lexicon of the New Testament and Other Early Christian Literature,* 2d ed. Revised and augmented by F. Wilbur Gingrich and Frederick W. Danker, from Walter Bauer's 5th ed., 1958 (Chicago, Ill.: University of Chicago Press, 1979), pp. 503–4.

source of spiritual life and nourishment. Unless we abide in Him, the spiritual life is barren.

> "Abide in Me, and I in you. As the branch cannot bear fruit of itself unless it abides in the vine, so neither can you unless you abide in Me. I am the vine, you are the branches; he who abides in Me and I in him, he bears much fruit; for apart from Me you can do nothing." (vv. 4–5)

Notice that the emphasis is on fruit-bearing—the abundant life of Christ reproduced in the lives of His followers. Fruit can't grow on a branch that has been severed from its source of life. Yet how often do we try to live spiritually separated from Christ? We often act the part—use Christian jargon, fill the pews on Sunday, tote our Bibles—while avoiding His presence and ignoring His Word. So we sever ourselves from the Vine. Oh, we may display a form of Christlikeness. But close inspection reveals only wax fruit.

Every vine needs a *vinedresser* to keep it pruned and productive.

> "I am the true vine, and My Father is the vine-dresser. Every branch in Me that does not bear fruit, He takes away; and every branch that bears fruit, He prunes it, so that it may bear more fruit." (vv. 1–2)

As the Vinedresser, our heavenly Father keeps the branches of the Vine in fruit-bearing shape. He "takes away" those that are not bearing fruit. That doesn't mean He discards them. In fact, it means just the opposite. The Greek word means "to raise, take up, lift." Our Lord looks for those branches not producing fruit, picks them out of the dirt, cleans them off, then hangs them back on the trellis where they can receive maximum sunlight.[2]

He also prunes those branches that are already productive so they can produce more fruit. Pruning, as Merrill Tenney states, can make the difference between a skimpy harvest and a bumper crop of grapes.

---

2. Commentator Elmer Towns explains: "Theologians debate the unfruitful branch which is apparently cast away. . . . [The] probable solution is seen in the word *airei* (taketh away). This word is the root for *resurrection* (to take up). The focus here is fruitbearing; the vinedresser does not cut away a vine because it has no fruit but gently lifts it up to the sun so it has an opportunity to bear fruit. The first step of Christ is not judgment but encouragement." *The Gospel of John: Believe and Live* (Old Tappan, N.J.: Fleming H. Revell Co., 1990), pp. 273–74.

> Every vineyard must be pruned by an expert. The vinedresser had to know how and when to prune and fertilize the vine, so that it would produce the maximum crop. . . .
>
> . . . In pruning a vine, two principles are generally observed: first, all dead wood must be ruthlessly removed; and second, the live wood must be cut back drastically. Dead wood harbors insects and disease and may cause the vine to rot, to say nothing of being unproductive and unsightly. Live wood must be trimmed back in order to prevent such heavy growth that the life of the vine goes into the wood rather than into fruit. The vineyards in the early spring look like a collection of barren, bleeding stumps; but in the fall they are filled with luxuriant purple grapes.[3]

Likewise, the Vinedresser takes His pruning knife to us, cutting away all that will hinder the growth of fruit.

Finally, let's take a closer look at the *branches*, which represent believers.

> "Abide in Me, and I in you. As the branch cannot bear fruit of itself unless it abides in the vine, so neither can you unless you abide in Me. I am the vine, you are the branches; he who abides in Me, and I in him, he bears much fruit; for apart from Me you can do nothing. If anyone does not abide in Me, he is thrown away as a branch and dries up; and they gather them, and cast them into the fire and they are burned. If you abide in Me, and My words abide in you, ask whatever you wish, and it shall be done for you." (vv. 4–7)

Did you notice that we're not *directly* commanded to bear fruit? We're told to abide; that's our primary responsibility. We're to stay close to Christ. Depend on Him. Draw strength from Him. Let His life flow through us. Only then will the fruit come. Knowing about the fruit, though, gives us a measuring stick with which to check ourselves to ensure that we are indeed abiding.

3. Merrill C. Tenney, *John: The Gospel of Belief* (Grand Rapids, Mich.: William B. Eerdmans Publishing Co., 1948), p. 227.

We need to know that God wants us to "abide in" Him, but we also need to realize that "abiding in" Him means we'll exhibit "love, joy, peace, patience, kindness, goodness, faithfulness, gentleness, self-control" (Gal. 5:22–23), as well as moral excellence, knowledge, perseverance, godliness, and brotherly kindness (2 Pet. 1:5–7). Do you see how helpful knowledge of the fruit can be? Knowing specifically what the fruit is gives us a clearer picture of what abiding means. If God had wanted us to ignore the fruit—to treat it as some kind of unimportant by-product—He would not have listed them in the Bible. He wants us to know them so we'll know for sure whether we're abiding in Christ.

We need to hear that. Frankly, we can do many things without depending on Christ. We can run a business or run a church. We can busy ourselves with all kinds of ministry. But if He's not the source of all we do, there will be no real fruit. There will be a mechanical superficiality to our lives. Apart from Him, we can "do nothing" (v. 5).

Not abiding can lead to severe consequences—being "thrown away" by God (v. 6). This doesn't mean believers lose their salvation, but it does mean that God may remove us from ministry, even take us in physical death, if we refuse to stay connected to Him.

Well, if we don't lose our salvation, what does "cast them into the fire" mean? The switch to plural ("them") here provides us a clue.

> In the first half of verse 6, Jesus has used the singular *he* to refer to the branch. But notice in the second half, when it comes to the severity of judgment, He states everything in the plural. "They gather them . . . cast them . . . they are burned." "He" is thrown away, but "they" are cast in the fire. Meaning what? With the change to the plural, the focus moves away from the person and onto the fruits of that person's carnal life. The branch is cut off by divine discipline and the bitter fruits of the flesh that the branch was producing are burned up.[4] (See also 1 Cor. 3:12–15.)

Don't despair, though. Look at the good in store for those who do abide:

---

4. From the study guide *His Name Is Wonderful,* coauthored by Lee Hough, from the Bible-teaching ministry of Charles R. Swindoll (Anaheim, Calif.: Insight for Living, 1992), p. 58.

- *Our prayers will be answered* (John 15:7). Far from a "name it, claim it" promise, this is assurance that we'll receive all we need when we're abiding in the Vine. Implied here is the fact that if we're abiding, we'll pray to honor God, not merely to satisfy our selfish desires.

- *God will be glorified* (v. 8). The more we abide, the more fruit we bear. And the more people will notice that we're Christ's followers.

- *Love will be stimulated* (vv. 9–10). If we abide in Christ, we'll be entwined in a love relationship with Him, which will also wrap around the lives of others.

- *Joy will overflow* (v. 11). Abiding in Christ brings real joy, not just temporary "warm fuzzies." Close connection with Jesus supplies us with a delight in living that withstands the harsh weather brought by painful circumstances.

Contrasting Responses to the Message

There are only two responses to a message like this. One is *refusal to abide, which leads to barrenness*. We break away. Go out on our own. Wing it. Stop consulting Christ for major decisions. Try to assemble a workable spiritual life without His instructions, apart from His Spirit.

The second is *willingness to abide, which leads to fruitfulness*. We stay connected to the Vine. Walk closely with Him. Depend on Him. Absorb His Word.

We can either be laden with clusters of ripe grapes, ready for harvesting, or barren as a brittle limb, waiting to be snapped off and pitched into the kindling pile.

"Abide," says Jesus. It's the only way to grow.

Living Insights

In one sense, we can never be disconnected from the Vine. Jesus Christ saved us, and He keeps us saved (John 10:27–29). But we live in a world full of false "vines" that try to convince us to break away from Christ and attach to something that seems more pleasurable, more immediate, less painful.

Temptation gnaws at our leaves like a hungry insect. Relational conflict and unforeseen catastrophes bite into our bark like the teeth of a saw. And sometimes we're close to snapping under the weight of legalism or religious busyness.

Is there anything tugging at the branches of your life, pulling you away from the Vine? Are you abiding enough to bear fruit? List one thing that might be slowing down your fruit production.

_____

_____

_____

_____

_____

How do you think the Vinedresser can help you prune it back so that you can abide more deeply and bear more fruit?

_____

_____

_____

_____

_____

Here's to a robust harvest!

Chapter 7

RESTING IN CHRIST
Matthew 11:28–30

What one word would best describe how your life feels most of the time? *Stressed? Hurried? Harried? Pressured? Behind? Restful? Restful?* This one doesn't seem to fit, does it? If we judge the state of our society by the top prescribed medications, we know that *restful* isn't the overarching truth for most of us. What are the top medications? Prozac, used to treat depression, and Tagamet, used to treat stomach and intestinal ulcers.

We are one uptight, exhausted, stressed-out, anxiety-ridden, burned-out culture. And we sure need a breather.

Jesus knows this even better than we do. To all of us who are taking a beating from life, He extends a gracious invitation. Better than just a breather, He offers a whole new lifestyle that has His rest at its core.

> "Come to Me, all who are weary and heavy-laden,
> and I will give you rest. Take My yoke upon you and
> learn from Me, for I am gentle and humble in heart,
> and you will find rest for your souls. For My yoke is
> easy and My burden is light." (Matt. 11:28–30)

O gentle Savior! Let's take hold of His outstretched hand and take to heart each phrase of His kindly offer.

"Come to Me"

First, notice that Christ invites us to come to *Him*. He's the answer for our fatigued spirits. "I am the door," Jesus said, "if anyone enters through Me, he will be saved" (John 10:9). Jesus is the only door through which we can enter God's rest.

So often we try to find relief through other means. Christians sometimes substitute the church for Christ, while others seek different religions or cults, like Buddhism or the New Age movement. Some try yoga or Tai Chi Chuan, trying to bring peace to the spirit through the body. Exercise can be physically and mentally helpful (1 Tim. 4:8), but spiritual rest must come through spiritual means — and the only true means is Christ. Coming to Jesus, believing in Him, is the first step to finding rest.

"All Who Are Weary and Heavy-Laden"

Who does Jesus invite to come to Him? *All* who are "weary and heavy-laden." Jesus excludes no one. He avails His rest to young and old, male and female, rich and poor, black and white, and every shade of color in between.

All may come to Him, especially those who are *weary* and *heavy-laden*. William Barclay renders this phrase, "all you who are exhausted and weighted down beneath your burdens."[1] What was burdening the people in Jesus' day? They were "fainting under the legal burden" of the Law and the Pharisees' interpretation of it.[2] Their faith had been turned into a system of Jewish legalism and pharisaical arrogance. Barclay explains that

> for the orthodox Jew religion was a thing of burdens. Jesus said of the Scribes and Pharisees: "They bind heavy burdens, hard to bear, and lay them on men's shoulders" (Matthew 23:4). To the Jew religion was a thing of endless rules. A man lived his life in a forest of regulations which dictated every action of his life. He must listen for ever to a voice which said, "Thou shalt not."[3]

Endless rules and "thou shalt nots" squash the life out of the soul. Unfortunately, we still live in a world of rules, rules, rules—whether they come from Christianity's version of legalism, from the pressures and expectations the world forces on us, or from the heavy judgments of others (or even ourselves). These rules and regulations are just as crushing now as they were then. Mercifully, to all of us who are spiritually drained, physically exhausted, or mentally stressed-out, Jesus offers relief.

"I Will Give You Rest"

The Greek term for *rest, anapauō,* means "to cause to cease, to

1. William Barclay, *The Gospel of Matthew*, rev. ed., The Daily Study Bible Series (Philadelphia, Pa.: Westminster Press, 1975), vol. 2, p. 15.

2. Gerhard Kittel and Gerhard Friedrich, eds., *Theological Dictionary of the New Testament*, translated and abridged in one volume by Geoffrey W. Bromiley (1985; reprint, Grand Rapids, Mich.: William B. Eerdmans Publishing Co., 1992), p. 453.

3. Barclay, *The Gospel of Matthew*, vol. 2, p. 16.

give rest, refresh."[4] It's used to describe physical rest (Mark 6:31), as well as emotional and spiritual refreshment (1 Cor. 16:18). It also carries the idea of relief, according to R. V. G. Tasker:

> *Rest* in verses 28 and 29 . . . would perhaps be more accurately, and less misleadingly, translated "relief." Certainly Jesus does not promise His disciples a life of inactivity or repose, nor freedom from sorrow and struggle, but He does assure them that, if they keep close to Him, they will find relief from such crushing burdens as crippling anxiety, the sense of frustration and futility, and the misery of a sin-laden conscience.[5]

Through Christ, we are reconciled to God, at peace with Him (Rom. 5:10; 2 Cor. 5:18–20; Eph. 2:13–18; Col. 1:13–23). We don't live by anxious rule-keeping but by faith (Rom. 1:17; Gal. 3:10–14). We no longer stagger under the crushing load of our sin but stand straight and free in Christ's forgiveness (Matt. 26:28; Acts 5:31; 10:43; 26:18). Because of Christ's new life in us, we can reenter our activities with renewed vigor and an understanding that God will give us the time and energy to accomplish His will through us.

"Take My Yoke upon You"

How could wearing a yoke possibly lead to rest? Well, it all depends on the type of yoke. If you were struggling under the yoke of the Law and the Pharisees' merciless take on it, then you would have no rest. But Jesus' yoke is different. It's not a license to run wild but a call to "the discipline of discipleship."[6] Christ isn't inviting us to become Christian couch potatoes! A yoke is for work, after all. And He has work for us to do, work that He comes alongside us to help with—the work of love (see Rom. 13:8–14; 1 Cor. 13; Gal. 5:13–14; 1 John 4:7–12, 21; 5:3)[7]. Jesus doesn't

---

4. Kittel and Friedrich, *Theological Dictionary of the New Testament*, abridged, p. 56.

5. R. V. G. Tasker, *The Gospel according to St. Matthew: An Introduction and Commentary*, Tyndale New Testament Commentaries series (1961; reprint, Grand Rapids, Mich.: William B. Eerdmans Publishing Co., 1981), p. 122.

6. D. A. Carson, "Matthew," in *The Expositor's Bible Commentary*, gen. ed. Frank E. Gaebelein (Grand Rapids, Mich.: Zondervan Publishing House, Regency Reference Library, 1984), vol. 8, p. 278.

7. See also 1 Corinthians 16:14; 2 Corinthians 5:14; Ephesians 2:10; 5:1–2; James 2:8.

give us more rules to follow; rather, He invites us to follow Him, the Lord of love, and learn from His instruction and example.

"Learn from Me"

Eugene Peterson, in *The Message*, paraphrases Jesus' words insightfully, "Walk with me and work with me—watch how I do it. Learn the unforced rhythms of grace."[8]

When we study Jesus as His student disciples, we learn

how to cope
  how to pray
    how to forgive
      how to tell the truth
        how to handle pressure
          how to stay close to the Father
            how to treat people with love and grace

And He makes learning easy because He is "gentle and humble in heart."

"For I Am Gentle and Humble in Heart"

Jesus is a humble teacher who treats His pupils with gentleness. Many teachers and leaders act superior toward their students and condescend to those "below" them. At worst, they make their pupils feel stupid and discourage them from learning. Jesus, however, has no desire to dominate; He came to serve (Matt. 20:28; Mark 10:42–45; John 13:1–17; Phil. 2:7). With this servant attitude, He patiently and gently prods us toward righteousness and good works.

Interestingly, with these servant qualities, Jesus would have also reinforced for His listeners that He was indeed their promised Messiah (see Isa. 42:1–3a; 53:1–7; Zech. 9:9). Who else but the Messiah could bring rest to people's very souls?

"You Will Find Rest for Your Souls"

Jesus borrows the phrase "You will find rest for your souls" (Matt. 11:29b) from a passage in Jeremiah 6:

Thus says the Lord,

---

8. Eugene H. Peterson, *The Message: The New Testament in Contemporary English* (Colorado Springs, Colo.: NavPress, 1993), p. 31.

"Stand by the ways and see and ask for the
   ancient paths,
Where the good way is, and walk in it;
And you will find rest for your souls." (v. 16a)

Our rest, then, in Jeremiah's words, "comes from returning to
God and faithfulness to the will of God"—which, in Jesus' words,
is the same as taking His yoke and learning to become gentle and
humble like Him.[9]

"My Yoke Is Easy and My Burden Is Light"

Jesus' final words in this passage parallel His gentleness and
humility: "For My yoke is easy and My burden is light" (Matt.
11:30). The Greek word for *easy*, *chrēstos*, means "good, kind," and
points to the divine kindness of God's patient grace.[10] Linked with
the image of the yoke, it also carries the idea of something that is
"well-fitting," as Barclay explains.

> In Palestine ox-yokes were made of wood; the ox
> was brought, and the measurements were taken. The
> yoke was then roughed out, and the ox was brought
> back to have the yoke tried on. The yoke was care-
> fully adjusted, so that it would fit well, and not gall
> the neck of the patient beast.[11]

Jesus' yoke is not galling but fits well, making it pleasant to work
in. Likewise, His burden is "light," not something to drag us down
and sap our strength, but something that is easy to bear. Jesus is telling
us that our participation in His life will be a joy and not a chore!
   Want to rest in Christ? Accept His offer—come to Him, take
His yoke upon you, and see how easy and light life can be with
God's majestic Son at your side.

---

9. David Hill, ed., *The Gospel of Matthew*, New Century Bible Series (1972; reprint, Green-
wood, S.C.: Attic Press, 1977), p. 208. D. A. Carson adds, "The entire verse is steeped in
OT language . . . but if this is intended to be not just an allusion but a fulfillment passage,
then Jesus is saying that 'the ancient paths' and 'the good way' . . . lie in taking on his
yoke because he is the one to whom the OT Scriptures point." "Matthew," *Expositor's Bible
Commentary*, p. 278.

10. Kittel and Friedrich, *Theological Dictionary of the New Testament*, abridged, pp. 1320–21.

11. Barclay, *The Gospel of Matthew*, vol. 2, p. 17.

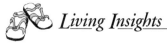 *Living Insights*

How is Jesus uniquely qualified to give us rest? We find a clue in the prayer He offered just before His invitation:

> "I praise You, Father, Lord of heaven and earth, that You have hidden these things from the wise and intelligent and have revealed them to infants. Yes, Father, for this way was well-pleasing in Your sight. All things have been handed over to Me by My Father; and no one knows the Son except the Father; nor does anyone know the Father except the Son, and anyone to whom the Son wills to reveal Him." (Matt. 11:25–27)

The Father has handed to Jesus "all things"—the knowledge of the Father, His eternal plans, and the empowerment to reveal that knowledge to whomever Jesus wants. This isn't just head knowledge; it is the heartbeat of the gospel. As R. V. G. Tasker noted, Jesus knows and discloses to us "the entire truth about the Father's redeeming love."[12]

Redeeming love—from the God of love (1 John 4:8, 16), through the Son, with love (John 3:16).

Jesus gives us rest from rules and regulations, expectations and judgments, because His single law is the law of love. Look at some of the areas this single law impacts:

- Love does no wrong to a neighbor (Rom. 13:10).

- Love looks out for others' interests (Phil. 2:4).

- Love lives in the truth (1 Cor. 13:6).

- Love takes compassionate action on behalf of the vulnerable (1 John 3:17–18).

- Love builds up others and seeks peace (Rom. 14:15, 19–20).

- Love frees us to care for each others' needs (Gal. 5:13).

- Love holds onto hope (Rom. 5:5).

12. Tasker, *The Gospel according to St. Matthew*, p. 121.

When we come to Christ and receive His love, that love of His fills and lightens our hearts. It displaces burdensome resentments and fears with forgiveness and trust. It supplants oppressive anger with understanding. It replaces the weight of guilt with the wings of grace. Love opens the door that lets Jesus' rest come streaming in.

What is burdening you, wearing you down, robbing you of rest? Health worries? Financial problems? Dreams that grow more distant with each passing day? Conflicts with your spouse or ex-spouse? Unrealistic expectations from your boss? Describe a few.

_____

_____

_____

_____

_____

_____

_____

How do you usually try to find relief? By tuning into television and tuning out your world? By overeating? By trying to control everything and everyone around you? By trying to be "perfect"? Even as Christians, we have ingrained ways of dealing with life that we learned from our families. What are some of yours?

_____

_____

_____

_____

_____

_____

How would your situation change if Christ's love were your guiding principle? Choose just one thing that's burdening you right now, and think through your motives, your feelings, and your responses. How would Christ's love impact each area?

_____

_____

_____

_____

_____

_____

_____

_____

"Come to Me . . . take My yoke . . . learn from Me," Jesus said, "and I will give you rest" (Matt. 11:28–29). How do we do this? By heeding His one law: "This is My commandment, that you love one another, just as I have loved you" (John 15:12).

Chapter 8

IT IS BEST TO REST

Hebrews 4:1–11

Even with as gracious an offer as Christ's (Matt. 11:28–30), many of us still find it difficult to truly rest. Why is that? Do we not believe what Jesus said? Is it too hard to trust in something spiritual that we can't see, hear, and touch?

Actually, the ancient Israelites had what they could see, hear, and touch, and they still missed out on the rest God offered. What happened? Let's follow the writer of Hebrews as he traces the Israelites' missteps so we can learn how to avoid their mistakes.

Israel's Folly

On the brink of the Promised Land, the grumbling, doubting people of Israel grumbled and doubted one time too many. They were so close too. Standing on the very banks of the Jordan with their toes in the water, they gazed upon the cornucopian land. Instead of becoming filled with faith, however, they filled up with fear—not fear of the God of heaven but of the giants in Canaan. As a result, their unbelief kept them from crossing that river and doomed them to become dust for the desert. Looking back, here's how the writer of Hebrews summarized this sad chapter in history:

> Take care, brethren, that there not be in any one of you an evil, unbelieving heart that falls away from the living God. . . . For who provoked Him when they had heard? Indeed, did not all those who came out of Egypt led by Moses? And with whom was He angry for forty years? Was it not with those who sinned, whose bodies fell in the wilderness? And to whom did He swear that they would not enter His rest, but to those who were disobedient? So we see that they were not able to enter because of unbelief. (Heb. 3:12, 16–19; see also vv. 7–11)

This chapter has been adapted from "Stop Churning and Start Resting" in the study guide *The Preeminent Person of Christ: A Study of Hebrews 1–10*, coauthored by Ken Gire, from the Bible-teaching ministry of Charles R. Swindoll (Fullerton, Calif.: Insight for Living, 1989).

That wilderness landscape is not a picture you'd want to hang over your sofa. True, in the background, just over the horizon, there's a land flowing with milk and honey. But in the foreground are the bloated corpses of the hard-hearted. Circling overhead in descending spirals are the vultures. And all the while, the blazing sun glares down with its unrelenting and unsympathetic stare.

What a tragedy! One the author of Hebrews hopes won't be repeated in our lives.

God's Offer

With this graphic picture of Israel's folly in mind, the writer issues his warning.

The Warning

Therefore, let us fear if, while a promise remains of entering His rest, any one of you may seem to have come short of it. (4:1)

Just as the gilded land of promise stretched before the Israelites, so God's rest stretches before us as a golden opportunity. But our entering is not automatic.

Before we go any further, let's define what we mean by *rest* in this context. The Greek term is *katapausis,* and it refers "to the rest (or resting place) that God gives to his people."[1] Rather than a physical place, like the Promised Land, the rest offered to us is spiritual and will be fully realized when Christ puts things right at the end of time.[2] However, we can certainly taste of it now, as we learned previously from Christ's offer of rest (Matt. 11:28–30). For practical purposes, then, we might call it *God's specially provided resting space.*

The Explanation

An explanation of this resting space is given in Hebrews 4:2–8. Let's take it point by point.

---

1. Gerhard Kittel and Gerhard Friedrich, eds., *Theological Dictionary of the New Testament,* translated and abridged in one volume by Geoffrey W. Bromiley (1985; reprint, Grand Rapids, Mich.: William B. Eerdmans Publishing Co., 1992), p. 420.

2. Henry T. C. Sun, "Rest; Resting Place," in *The International Standard Bible Encyclopedia,* rev. ed., gen. ed. Geoffrey W. Bromiley (Grand Rapids, Mich.: William B. Eerdmans Publishing Co., 1988), vol. 4, p. 144.

First, *entering God's rest takes the right formula.*

> For indeed we have had good news preached to us, just as they also; but the word they heard did not profit them, because it was not united by faith in those who heard. For we who have believed enter that rest, just as He has said,
> "As I swore in My wrath,
> They shall not enter My rest,"
> although His works were finished from the foundation of the world. (vv. 2–3)

Couched within these two verses is a simple formula:

Hearing + Believing = Resting

If we ignore the formula, we'll have no rest. Preaching the Word is essential, but unless faith in Jesus Christ follows the hearing of it, the result can be lethal. Merely attending a church that preaches the Bible isn't enough. The hearts that hear must be fertile and receptive to the seed that is sown (see Matt. 13:1–23).

Second, *entering God's rest takes the right attitude.*

> For He has said somewhere concerning the seventh day: "And God rested on the seventh day from all His works"; and again in this passage, "They shall not enter My rest." Therefore, since it remains for some to enter it, and those who formerly had good news preached to them failed to enter because of disobedience. (Heb. 4:4–6)

In this section, the writer goes all the way back to Creation, quoting from Genesis 2:2. God Himself established the pattern of rest when He worked six days and rested on the seventh. The first six days of Creation are marked off by the phrase "evening and . . . morning" (Gen. 1:5, 8, 13, 19, 23, 31). However, when we come to the seventh day, there are no time boundaries (2:1–3). There is also no mention of work on subsequent days. Meaning what? Meaning His Sabbath rest continues today.[3]

And God never intended to enjoy His special rest alone. He

---

3. See William Barclay, *The Letter to the Hebrews*, rev. ed., The Daily Study Bible Series (Philadelphia, Pa.: Westminster Press, 1976), p. 36.

left the gate open to those green pastures of repose for all who would soften their hearts to Him

The Israelites of Moses' generation, however, "failed to enter" God's physical rest in the Promised Land "because of disobedience." Their history also shows that most of them missed out on God's spiritual rest because of disobedience and faithlessness. Their lesson to us is to take God at His word and trust Him, because when we do, we live in the foretaste of that great heavenly banquet to which He Himself has invited us (Rev. 19:7–9).

Third, *entering God's rest takes the right time.*

> He again fixes a certain day, "Today," saying through
> David after so long a time just as has been said before,
> "Today if you hear His voice,
> Do not harden your hearts."
> For if Joshua had given them rest, He would not
> have spoken of another day after that. (Heb. 4:7–8)

Twice in these verses the writer stresses the urgency of entering into God's rest with the word *today*. The time is now, and He urges us not to put Him off. Practically speaking, every morning when we awaken, whether to sunshine or to gloom, we should start the day with God—before our feet even hit the floor!

The Availability

> So there remains a Sabbath rest for the people of God. For the one who has entered His rest has himself also rested from his works, as God did from His. (vv. 9–10)

The same rest God entered into after Creation "remains" for us. In trying to convey the idea of this rest, the writer of Hebrews coined a new word: *sabbatismos,* "Sabbath-rest."[4] Leon Morris explains that our connection to God's Sabbath rest pertains to both the present and the future.

> It is true of the here and now, for those who put their trust in Christ and His finished work do indeed rest from their own work. For them there is no striving

---

4. Leon Morris, "Hebrews," in *The Expositor's Bible Commentary,* gen. ed. Frank E. Gaebelein (Grand Rapids, Mich.: Zondervan Publishing House, Regency Reference Library, 1981), vol. 12, p. 42.

to achieve salvation through their own efforts but a quiet resting in what God has done for them. And it is true of the future, for in the world to come those who are in Christ enter a rest from this world's strivings, a rest from all their work. In both cases it can be said that we rest from our work "just as God did from his."[5]

The Command

Verse 11 gives direct counsel to those of us who have a difficult time entering a lifestyle of rest.

> Therefore let us be diligent to enter that rest, so that no one will fall, through following the same example of disobedience. (v. 11)

At first glance, the exhortation to be diligent to rest sounds like working hard to take a nap! It sounds contradictory, doesn't it? It even seems a little like we should be doing something to achieve our own salvation, yet we know that God has already done all the work for us. Walter A. Henrichsen helps unravel our confusion.

> The effort referred to here is the effort of faith (v. 11). It is hard to believe the promises of God. Why? Because they appear too good to be true. God says all we have to do is *confess* our sins to be forgiven (1 John 1:9). It is hard for us to forgive ourselves, much less to comprehend that we can be forgiven by a perfect God. God says we are to seek His kingdom, and He will assume responsibility for all our needs (Matt. 6:33). It is hard for us to believe that our daily needs do not have to be our number-one priority. We have to work at believing God.[6]

This is just what the Israelites didn't do, and through their disobedience and doubt they lost out on God's rest. Let's learn from them and work at cultivating our faith and entering fully into the joy God has for us.

5. Leon Morris, *Hebrews*, Bible Study Commentary Series (Grand Rapids, Mich.: Zondervan Publishing House, Lamplighter Books, 1983), p. 46.

6. Walter A. Henrichsen, *After the Sacrifice: A Practical Study of Hebrews* (Grand Rapids, Mich.: Zondervan Publishing House, Lamplighter Books, 1979), pp. 54–55.

Rest Provided

Along life's often troubled path, we'll encounter three barriers to rest: *presumption, panic,* and *pride.* We become *presumptuous* when we feel we've got things all figured out, when we think we can second-guess God and how He's going to resolve our problems. We become *panicked* when we feel we're not going to make it and start seeing ourselves as grasshoppers and our problems as giants (Num. 13:32–33). We become *prideful* when we feel we can handle life's problems without Jesus' or anybody else's help and try to pull ourselves up by our own bootstraps instead of reaching out to God's hand.

What can we do to overcome these barriers? Here's some simple —but not easy-to-follow—advice:

- *Resist presumption.* Make David's prayer your own, "Keep back Your servant from presumptuous sins" (Ps. 19:13).

- *Refuse to panic.* Remember that with God, nothing is too big or impossible (Luke 1:37).

- *Release your pride.* God helps, not those who help themselves, but those who cry out to Him (Deut. 33:26–27; Ps. 146:5, 8–9; Isa. 41:10, 13).

"Come to Me," Jesus promised, "and I will give you rest" (Matt. 11:28). "Be diligent," then, the writer to the Hebrews urges us, "to enter that rest" (Heb. 4:11). Let's do all we can to not miss one bit of the peace, rest, and joy Jesus has for us now and in eternity.

Living Insights

If you thought you were done resting, think again! It's time to make this personal. Psalm 46:10 reveals another facet of resting that hits close to home for all of us:

"Cease striving and know that I am God."

"Cease striving" is one word in Hebrew, *raphah.* It means "relax" or "withdraw."[7] It suggests inactivity, reminding us to withdraw from our own efforts and rely on God's strength. We might tell ourselves, "Stop straining in your own power and look to God."

7. Francis Brown, S. R. Driver, and Charles A. Briggs, *The New Brown-Driver-Briggs-Gesenius Hebrew and English Lexicon* (Peabody, Mass.: Hendrickson Publishers, 1979), p. 951.

We human beings, however, tend to be "control freaks." Like two-year-olds with a security blanket, we clutch our lives tightly, refusing to relinquish the right to make our own choices as we see fit. If we succeed, we credit our own smarts and talent. If we fail, we manage to find some comfort in having at least done it our way. We take pride in our autonomy.

This kind of self-important pride, though, turns us away from God rather than allowing us to cooperate with His plans—which are always better for us than our ideas are. This brings us to one of the great challenges of the Christian life: to release control to God and rest in Him.

Are you striving about something right now? List the decisions, relationships, and personal struggles that you have too tight a grip on.

_____

_____

_____

_____

Think about what you have coming up in the next few days, the next few hours. See anything else you need to "cease striving" from?

_____

_____

_____

Now take some time to know who God is. What attributes of His remind you that He is more than capable of taking care of you? Jot down the Scripture references that come to mind.

_____

_____

_____

_____

Finally, spend some time in prayerful surrender. In fact, make this a habit. Release your fears and concerns to God's majestic Son and start experiencing His rest.

Chapter 9

THE ABSOLUTE POWER OF JESUS OUR LORD

Selected Scriptures from John

Abundant, abiding, restful life. It sounds so good, doesn't it? It would be such a relief. Who wouldn't reach out for peace, for joy, for hope? But inside a lot of us, a small, sad voice keeps whispering something that keeps our stomachs knotted and our muscles in spasms. What's it saying? *If only . . . if only . . .*

If only my child would come back to God, then I could rest in Christ . . . If only my marriage was happy, then I could know Christ's abundant life . . . If only I had a more fulfilling job, then I'd know Christ's peace . . .

If only . . . if only . . .

You've tried everything you can, but you just can't change the situation. You've run smack-dab into a human impossibility. All of us do. Our mistake, though, is to think that a human impossibility is also an impossibility for God. God's track record, however, tells us just the opposite.

God brought Noah, his family, and all the creatures with him in the ark safely through the storm to dry land (Gen. 7–8). God parted the waters of the Red Sea and led Moses and His people through it while He wiped out their enemies, who thought they had the Israelites cornered (Exod. 13:17–14:31). God guided the stone from young David's slingshot so that with one hit between the eyes, the mighty Goliath fell dead (1 Sam. 17). God so loved the world that He rolled away the stone and gave us a bright Easter morning, raising Christ from the dead so that we, too, could have new life in Him (John 20; Rom. 6).

Human impossibilities are God's opportunities! Someone once said that we are all faced with a series of great opportunities, brilliantly disguised as impossible situations. These great, humanly insurmountable circumstances are God's opportunities to show His power, mercy, and love for us. He and His prophets have been telling us this for centuries:

> "'Ah Lord God! Behold, You have made the heavens and the earth by Your great power and by Your

outstretched arm! Nothing is too difficult for You.'"
(Jer. 32:17)

"Behold, I am the Lord, the God of all flesh; is anything too difficult for Me?" (v. 27)

"For nothing will be impossible with God." (Luke 1:37)

But [Jesus] said, "The things that are impossible with people are possible with God." (18:27)

Nothing is too difficult, let alone impossible, for God. And the same goes for His Son. Let's observe two truths about Jesus' power, then we'll look at seven events John recorded in his Gospel that reveal our Lord to be the ultimate impossibility opportunist.

Two Observations

First, *our Lord's power is absolutely unlimited*. After His resurrection, Jesus told His disciples, "All authority has been given to Me in heaven and on earth" (Matt. 28:18). What does this mean for us? That Jesus has more power than any of our enemies. That He has authority over biopsy tests and CAT scans. Nothing lies beyond His jurisdiction and control.

Second, *our Lord's promise is totally unconditional*. Jesus does not restrict His help only to those of a certain age, sex, or race. Neither does He withhold aid from people who are imperfect, unpleasant, or even criminal. Didn't Jesus say, "Come to Me, *all* who are weary and heavy-laden, and I will give you rest" (11:28, emphasis added)? Yes, He avails His help to everyone.

Seven "Impossible" Situations

Jesus spoke with His actions as much as His words. John records seven events in which Jesus proclaimed His power over impossibilities. Through these seven miracles, Jesus not only demonstrated His dominance over temporal problems but also identified Himself as the only One who could solve humanity's eternal dilemma—death and eternal separation from God. Only by believing in Him can we receive eternal life. And only by continuing to trust in Him can He help us through our current problems. Let's look, then, at Jesus' power over seven impossibilities.

Water into Wine

Jesus first showed His power in the realm of *quality*. Mary, Jesus, and His disciples had been invited to a wedding in Cana, but the wine for the celebration had run out (John 2:1–3a). On the surface, running out of wine seems like a mild problem, hardly worthy of being called an impossibility. Leon Morris, however, reveals that a grave danger lay behind this seemingly superficial problem.

> This meant more than the disruption of the festivities. There was something of a slur on the hosts, for they had not fully discharged the duties of hospitality. This may indicate that they were poor and had made the minimum provision, hoping for the best. It is also possible that the lack of wine involved another embarrassment, in that it rendered the bridegroom's family liable to a lawsuit. They were legally required to provide a feast of a certain standard.[1]

With the bridegroom's honor and financial future on the line, Jesus agreed to help. He had some servants fill six stone waterpots, which were used for ritual purification purposes, with water—about "twenty or thirty gallons each" (vv. 3b–7). Then He had some ladled out and brought to the headwaiter, who exclaimed,

> "Every man serves the good wine first, and when the people have drunk freely, then he serves the poorer wine; but you have kept the good wine until now." (v. 10)

Jesus transformed the water into the best of wine! What is He trying to teach us with this sign? That He has transforming power—He can change the quality of our lives. Morris observes three changes this sign points to:

> He changes the water of Judaism into the wine of Christianity, the water of Christlessness into the wine of the richness and the fullness of eternal life in Christ, the water of the law into the wine of the gospel.[2]

1. Leon Morris, *The Gospel according to John*, rev. ed., The New International Commentary on the New Testament series (Grand Rapids, Mich.: William B. Eerdmans Publishing Co., 1995), pp. 157–58.

2. Morris, *The Gospel according to John*, p. 155.

He will fill our emptiness with joy, hope, love, and eternal life—things much more valuable and lasting than a glass of Bordeaux.

Healing the Official's Son

Jesus left Cana for awhile, ministering in Jerusalem and Samaria, but returned to the village of His first miracle to perform another sign that showed His power over *distance*. A royal official had a son who lay dying in Capernaum, a city about twenty miles away. This desperate father traveled all that distance to beg Jesus to return with him and heal his son (4:46–49). Jesus, however, rather than going with the official, simply told him, "Go; your son lives" (v. 50a).

The man took Jesus at His word and started home. On the way, his slaves brought him the good news that his son was alive and well—and the healing happened at the exact time Jesus told him that the boy was alive (vv. 50b–53a). As a result, "He himself believed, and his whole household" (v. 53).

Jesus doesn't have to be physically near to grace us with His healing power. To borrow the psalmist's words, He is "a very present help in trouble" (Ps. 46:1b). Although Jesus currently sits enthroned at His Father's right hand in heaven, He can still intervene in our lives. He has power over distance, and He's only a prayer away.

Healing at Bethesda

Sometime after healing the official's son, Jesus headed for Jerusalem to celebrate the Passover. As He walked the streets of that ancient city, He came across a sad sight: "a multitude of those who were sick, blind, lame, and withered" who were waiting for a miracle at the pool of Bethesda (John 5:1–4). One poor soul had been ill for thirty-eight years—but this day would change everything for him, because Jesus has the power over *time*.

Jesus made His way toward this man and asked an interesting question, "Do you wish to get well?" (v. 6). William Barclay offers this insight into Jesus' question:

> It was not so foolish a question as it may sound. The man had waited for thirty-eight years and it might well have been that hope had died and left behind a passive and dull despair. In his heart of hearts the man might be well content to remain an invalid for, if he was cured, he would have to shoulder all the burden of making a living. . . . But this man's response

was immediate. He wanted to be healed, though he did not see how he ever could be since he had no one to help him.

The first essential towards receiving the power of Jesus is to have intense desire for it. Jesus says: "Do you really want to be changed?" If in our inmost hearts we are well content to stay as we are, there can be no change for us.[3]

This man definitely wanted to change, and Jesus sensed that. So He told him, "'Get up, pick up your pallet, and walk.' Immediately the man became well, and picked up his pallet and began to walk" (vv. 8–9).

Thirty-eight years—nearly four decades. That's a long, long time to go without the use of your legs. It's a long time to depend on others to carry you around, a long time not to provide for yourself or your family. But Jesus overcame time. With a single sentence He ended the man's suffering and overcame his impossibility. Nothing we suffer from—no addiction, ailment, or conflict—is too entrenched for the power of God's majestic Son.

Feeding the Five Thousand

The next of Jesus' signs that John records shows His power over *quantity.* Jesus had been ministering to a large crowd on a mountain across the Sea of Galilee. As it was getting late, He looked at the mass of physically and spiritually hungry people and thought of a way to meet both of their needs. He hadn't, however, clued in His disciples on His plan. He asked Philip,

> "Where are we to buy bread, so that these may eat?" This He was saying to test him; for He Himself knew what He was intending to do. Philip answered Him, "Two hundred denarii worth of bread is not sufficient for them, for everyone to receive a little." One of His disciples, Andrew, Simon Peter's brother, said to Him, "There is a lad here who has five barley loaves and two fish, but what are these for so many people?" Jesus said, "Have the people sit down." (6:5–10a)

3. William Barclay, *The Gospel of John,* vol. 1, rev. ed., The Daily Study Bible Series (Philadelphia, Pa.: Westminster Press, 1975), p. 179.

The disciples felt overwhelmed at the prospect of feeding five thousand people. The sheer quantity of food required to satisfy everyone made the task impossible. Yet Jesus seized the opportunity and once again proved His power over our problems. Giving thanks for the loaves and fish, He took the little the disciples had and fed everyone—about five thousand men—and filled twelve baskets with leftovers (vv. 10b–13)! Nothing is too much for our Lord, or too little. Whether we're deep in debt or dusting bare cupboards, we can trust in the absolute, abundant power of Jesus our Lord to provide for us.

Walking on Water

Having watched their teacher perform these four miraculous wonders, the disciples were filled with unshakable, unsinkable faith, right? Wrong. Look at how they responded to Jesus' power over *nature*.

> Now when evening came, His disciples went down to the sea, and after getting into a boat, they started to cross the sea to Capernaum. It had already become dark, and Jesus had not yet come to them. The sea began to be stirred up because a strong wind was blowing. Then, when they had rowed about three or four miles, they saw Jesus walking on the sea and drawing near to the boat; and they were frightened. But He said to them, "It is I; do not be afraid."[4] (John 6:16–20)

It's safe to say that the disciples had not fully grasped what Jesus was telling them through His signs—the wine at Cana, the healing of the official's son, the compassionate curing of the lame man at Bethesda. They still did not see Jesus for who He was—the Messiah of the world and the overcomer of impossible situations.

All too often, neither do we. We, too, need to learn from the times God has intervened in our lives so that we can trust Him to handle whatever we're currently going through. And rather than being terrified by His power, we can be reassured by it.

---

4. John leaves out Peter's walk—and sink—that Matthew records (Matt. 14:28–31). And Mark tells us why the disciples were afraid and astonished: "They had not gained any insight from the incident of the loaves, but their heart was hardened" (Mark 6:52).

Healing the Man Born Blind

Jesus' next sign shows His power over *misfortune*. As Jesus escaped the Jewish religious leaders at the temple (8:59), He passed by a man who had been born blind (9:1). His disciples wanted to know whose fault this misfortune was, but Jesus explained,

> "It was neither that this man sinned, nor his parents; but it was so that the works of God might be displayed in him." (v. 3)

So the Light of the World made a clay poultice, applied it to the blind man's eyes, and brought him out of a lifetime of darkness (vv. 5–7). His neighbors could hardly believe it (vv. 8–12), and the Pharisees could hardly stand it—Jesus had performed this miracle, done this work, on the Sabbath (vv. 13–34).

Friend, if God wants to intervene in the most remarkable, unusual, unorthodox manner, don't debate it or demean it, just say, "Thank You" and throw a party!

And remember, this man's blindness was a misfortune, not a punishment. Many things are misfortunes: Down's Syndrome, paralyzation, and a host of other disabilities. Jesus is Lord over these impossibilities. He proved it to the blind man and the disciples, and He wants us to believe it too. He wants us to trust in Him when misfortune comes our way. If He doesn't heal, He always gives the power to endure.

Raising Lazarus

For His final statement of power, Jesus saved the best for last. His good friend Lazarus had fallen sick, and Lazarus' sisters, Martha and Mary, had sent word to Him. But Jesus, seeing an opportunity to build faith into the women and His disciples, chose to stay away and allow Lazarus to die (11:1–15).

When He finally made it to Lazarus, His friend had been dead for four days. The sisters were confused and grieved by Jesus' apparent lack of compassion (vv. 17–32). Seeing their grief, Jesus was "deeply moved in spirit and was troubled," and He wept with them (vv. 33–35). Then He ordered the grave opened, called forth His friend, and Lazarus walked out of the tomb (v. 44).

Jesus proved that He held sway over all things, even *death*. Why did He go through all this trouble? John gives us the reason:

> Therefore many other signs Jesus also performed

in the presence of the disciples, which are not written in this book; but these have been written so that you may believe that Jesus is the Christ, the Son of God; and that believing you may have life in His name. (20:30–31)

Believing to eternal life is Jesus' goal. It's the purpose for which He performed His miracles. He wanted His disciples to believe, and He also wants us to trust in Him so we have an opportunity to receive His love and concern.

"Is anything too difficult for Me?" the Lord asks (Jer. 32:27). Jesus' life answers, "Absolutely not!"

Living Insights

Jesus' greatest miracle, of course, was His final victory over death by rising from the grave. This final miracle validated every one He had done before, and it's the one through which He can offer us eternal life.

Jesus wants us to place our trust in Him. Without saving faith, frankly, none of our other problems really matter. Would you ask a carpenter to sand your dining table if the rest of the house was on fire? Similarly, it's ludicrous to ask Jesus to help you with a temporal problem if you haven't first settled your eternal destiny. If you haven't placed your trust in Him, take a moment to do so now through prayer.

With the most important issue taken care of, let's now move on to our temporal problems, to see how Jesus can help.

Which of Jesus' seven signs meant the most to you? Why?

_____

_____

_____

_____

Describe the difficulties you're currently facing.

_____

_____

This chapter showed us that Jesus holds sway over quality, distance, time, quantity, nature, misfortune, and death. Under which category do your problems fall?

_____

_____

_____

Pray to God now, in Jesus' name. Ask Him to help you. If it's not His will to remove your problems from you, ask Him to give you the strength and patience you need to bear up under the weight of your burden. Finally, place your trust in this promise from Jesus:

> "Ask, and it will be given to you; seek, and you will find; knock, and it will be opened to you. For everyone who asks receives, and he who seeks finds, and to him who knocks it will be opened. Or what man is there among you who, when his son asks for a loaf, will give him a stone? Or if he asks for a fish, he will not give him a snake, will he? If you then, being evil, know how to give good gifts to your children, how much more will your Father who is in heaven give what is good to those who ask Him!" (Matt. 7:7–11)

Chapter 10

OUR LORD'S
HEALING POWER

Selected Scriptures

As we saw in our previous chapter, three of John's seven signs involved Jesus' power to heal. With just the words, "Go; your son lives," Jesus brought the official's son back from the brink of death (John 4:46–53). With a question and a command, He then freed a man who was imprisoned for thirty-eight years within his own body: "Do you wish to get well? . . . Get up, pick up your pallet and walk" (5:2–9). A little later, with the unlikely elements of saliva and earth, the Light of the World dispelled the lifelong darkness of a man born blind, applying clay to his eyes and saying, "Go, wash in the pool of Siloam" (9:1–7).

Clearly, Jesus has both the power and the authority to heal. But do we? Does it logically follow that, if His life is abundantly in us, we, too, have His same power to heal? Should we be seeking to eradicate all illness and relieve all pain and suffering in the name of Christ? Has He imparted to us His abilities to divinely heal, making us divine healers?

Many people have been hurt by those claiming to be faith healers. The sick and needy have had emotional pain added to their physical suffering, had their tender trust in God torn to tatters. Is this God's will? Is this the desire of Jesus' gentle heart? Certainly not. His healing brings comfort and mercy and joy, not confusion and shame and more pain.

To bring clarity to the confusion over this issue, we need the sound and balanced teaching of God's Word. Let's begin by exploring God's power and prerogatives, then examine five laws of healing, and finally move on to specific teaching regarding healing from Jesus' brother, James.

God's Power and Prerogative

Basically, all of Scripture testifies that *God can do whatever He wishes, with whomever He chooses, at anytime He pleases.* He is all-powerful; and He is also sovereign, reserving the right to choose whom He will for whatever purpose delights and glorifies Him at whatever time He selects. Listen to the testimony of His Spirit-guided writers:

> Our God is in the heavens;
> He does whatever He pleases. (Ps. 115:3)

> For I know that the Lord is great
> And that our Lord is above all gods.
> Whatever the Lord pleases, He does,
> In heaven and in earth, in the seas and in all deeps.
> (135:5–6; see also Dan. 4:35)

It's also God's power and choice to heal, not His followers'. Two of Jesus' disciples, Peter and John, make this clear. When a lame beggar asked them for alms at the temple, Peter knew that God wanted to give this man much more.

> Peter said, "I do not possess silver and gold, but what I do have I give to you: In the name of Jesus Christ the Nazarene—walk!" (Acts 3:6)

The man not only walked, he leaped and praised God! But a crowd soon formed, looking with awe—at Peter and John. So Peter corrected them:

> "Men of Israel, why are you amazed at this, or why do you gaze at us, as if by our own power or piety we had made him walk? The God of Abraham, Isaac and Jacob the God of our fathers, has glorified His servant Jesus. . . . On the basis of faith in His name, it is the name of Jesus which has strengthened this man whom you see and know; and the faith which comes through Him has given him this perfect health in the presence of you all." (vv. 12–13a, 16)

In His sovereign power, God chose to heal this helpless beggar. And notice, when God heals, He heals immediately and permanently. It "takes" the first time, unlike the experiences many have with faith healers, who blame and shame people and absolve themselves of all responsibility when people aren't healed at their touch.

The power to heal is God's, and so is the choice to heal. Does that seem hard and cold? Does God seem unfair because He does "whatever He pleases"? He may *seem* unfair or even unloving by allowing pain and suffering to continue. But only if we think we deserve better. As we'll see in the next section, pain and suffering do not come from God; they come from sin, from humanity's own rebellion against Him. So God is actually merciful when He relieves us from the natural consequences of our fallen, human nature.

Now that we have this foundation established, let's build on it with five spiritual laws regarding physical healing.

Five Laws of Healing

By keeping the following truths in mind, we can save ourselves and others much heartache and disillusionment.[1]

Number one: *There are two categories of sin: original and personal.* Original sin refers to the sin nature we inherited from Adam (Rom. 5:12). Personal sin is the daily disobedience that is spawned by our Adamic nature (7:14–23; see also 3:23). Original sin is the root; personal sin is the fruit.

Number two: *Original sin introduced sickness, suffering, and death to the human race.* Had Adam and Eve never sinned, they never would have died. But because they disobeyed God, sickness and death spread to every living thing (Rom. 5:12). So, in the broadest sense, all sickness and death are the result of original sin.

Number three: *Sometimes there is a direct link between personal sins and sicknesses.* Paul attested to this when he chastised the Corinthian believers who were coming to the Lord's Table in an "unworthy manner" and being stricken by God's judgment (1 Cor. 11:27). He told them, "For this reason many among you are weak and sick, and a number sleep [have died]" (v. 30; see also Ps. 32:3–4; 38:1–8; John 5:14).

Number four: *Sometimes there is no link between personal sins and sicknesses.* Remember the exchange between Jesus and His disciples regarding the man born blind?

> His disciples asked Him, "Rabbi, who sinned, this man or his parents, that he would be born blind?" Jesus answered, "It was neither that this man sinned, nor his parents; but it was so that the works of God might be displayed in him." (John 9:2–3)

We need to take the disciples' lesson to heart and guard ourselves

---

1. The balance of this chapter and the Living Insights have been adapted from "Suffering, Sickness, Sin—and Healing," in the study guide *James . . . Practical and Authentic Living,* coauthored by Lee Hough, from the Bible-teaching ministry of Charles R. Swindoll (Fullerton, Calif.: Insight for Living, 1991).

from blaming a person's sins for his or her sickness. We don't always know the reasons, and we would be presumptuous to even pretend that we do.

Number five: *It is not God's will that everyone be healed.* Typically, those who claim that God wants everyone to be healed base their belief on a misunderstanding of Isaiah 53:5b: "By His scourging we are healed." The context of this verse, however, refers to the healing of the soul, not the body. Peter underscored this when he wrote,

> He Himself bore our sins in His body on the cross,
> so that we might die to sin and live to righteousness;
> for by His wounds you were healed. (1 Pet. 2:24)

Many people in Scripture were never healed supernaturally. Trophimus, for example, remained sick in Miletus, despite Paul's gift of healing (2 Tim. 4:20; compare Acts 20:9–12; 28:8–9). Timothy, Paul's spiritual son, had a stomach problem and "frequent ailments" (1 Tim. 5:23). And Paul himself was always plagued by his mysterious "thorn in the flesh," learning that living in God's grace was more important than being healed (2 Cor. 12:7–10).

These are the five laws from our manual of faith—God's Word. It's crucial that we form our opinions about healing from the theology of Scripture so we're grounded in the truth. That's the best way to avoid the pain of being misled and let down.

Scriptural Counsel from James

What is God's primary advice when we encounter suffering and sickness? In the final section of his letter, James reveals that it is prayer.

When We Are Suffering

"Is anyone among you suffering? Then he must pray" (James 5:13a). The Greek term for *suffering* here, *kakopatheō*, literally means "to suffer misfortune, to be in a sorry situation."[2] In this verse, it refers to the spiritual burden that a distressing situation brings with it.[3] So when we're burdened, distressed, in trouble, or afflicted, James

---

2. Gerhard Kittel and Gerhard Friedrich, eds., *Theological Dictionary of the New Testament,* translated and abridged in one volume by Geoffrey W. Bromiley (1985; reprint, Grand Rapids, Mich.: William B. Eerdmans Publishing Co., 1992), p. 803.

3. Wilhelm Michaelis, in the *Theological Dictionary of the New Testament,* ed. Gerhard Friedrich, trans. and ed. Geoffrey W. Bromiley (1967; reprint, Grand Rapids, Mich.: William B. Eerdmans Publishing Co., 1991), vol. 5, p. 937.

tells us, "Pray." Pray for endurance rather than escape (compare John 17:15). Pray for patience rather than a quick fix (1 Pet. 2:20). Pray for a gracious spirit rather than an irritated one (1 Cor. 13:5). Pray for wisdom and the willingness to let God do His work in your life (Phil. 2:13; James 1:2–5).

When We Are Happy

James next moves from those who suffer to those at the other end of the spectrum: "Is anyone cheerful? He is to sing praises" (5:13b). Essentially, James is saying that "if we are fortunate enough to be happy, we should thank God by singing songs of praise. . . . Singing is actually another form of prayer."[4] So when we're not experiencing hardship, we don't need to feel guilty. As Solomon observed, there is "a time to weep and a time to laugh; A time to mourn and a time to dance" (Eccles. 3:4). If we're joyful, James says to let it out! Sing praises and thank God for the blessings He has given.

When We Are Sick

Physical sickness is another area requiring prayer.

> Is anyone among you sick? Then he must call for the elders of the church and they are to pray over him, anointing him with oil in the name of the Lord. (James 5:14)

The Greek term for sick used here, *astheneō*, means "to be weak, feeble" and comes from a root (*asthenēs*) meaning "without strength." "The sick person here," Barton, Veerman, and Wilson tell us, "is incapacitated physically."[5] What does James recommend in this situation?

First, the person who is sick should take the initiative and summon the elders of the church. No one can know we're sick unless we tell them. So, when we become seriously ill, our first step is to make others aware of our needs.

Second, the elders are to anoint and pray over the person.[6]

4. Bruce B. Barton, David R. Veerman, and Neil Wilson, *James*, Life Application Bible Commentary Series (Wheaton, Ill.: Tyndale House Publishers, 1992), p. 137.

5. Barton, Veerman, and Wilson, *James*, p. 138.

6. Some people have taken this verse to mean that the clergy, namely priests, should administer last rites to the dying using oil and a special liturgy. However, this passage concerns restoring to health, not dying. Others think this verse applies only to the first-century apostles. James, however, addressed "elders," not apostles; therefore, it still applies.

According to the Greek construction of the sentence, the verse actually states: "Let them pray over him, having anointed him with oil in the name of the Lord." The anointing, then, should precede the praying. What type of anointing is this? Jay Adams explains.

> The ordinary word for a ceremonial anointing was *chrio* (a cognate of *christos* [Christ] the "anointed One"). The word James used *(aleipho)*, in contrast to the word *chrio* ("to anoint"), usually means "to rub" or simply "apply." The word *aleipho* was used to describe the personal application of salves, lotions, and perfumes, which usually had an oil base. . . . *Aleipho* was used frequently in medical treatises. And so it turns out that what James required by the use of oil was the use of the best medical means of the day . . . accompanied by prayer. The two are to be used together; neither to the exclusion of the other. So instead of teaching faith healing apart from the use of medicine, the passage teaches just the opposite.[7]

Elders today, in light of this historical insight into James' counsel, should ask the sick person, "Have you sought the advice of your physician—and are you following doctor's orders?" Medicine is a gift from God, and ignoring it to show that we trust God isn't really trust at all—it's spurning His provision.

Third, the elders are to pray (James 5:14b). As believers we should only pray for God's will to be done, not ours (compare 4:3). God may use the medicine to cure the illness . . . or He may not. We have to leave the results in His hands and stay close to Him in humble, faithful prayer.

James next touches on the link between sin and sickness.

> The prayer offered in faith will restore the one who is sick, and the Lord will raise him up, and if he has committed sins, they will be forgiven him. Therefore, confess your sins to one another, and pray for one another so that you may be healed. The effective prayer of a righteous man can accomplish much. (5:15–16)

---

7. Jay E. Adams, *Competent to Counsel* (Grand Rapids, Mich.: Baker Book House, 1970), pp. 107–8. For biblical examples of oil's medicinal uses, see Isaiah 1:6 and Luke 10:33–34.

If it's part of God's sovereign purpose to heal a person in this earthly life, then He will do it. He will raise that person from the sickbed; and if the illness is sin-related, He will respond to that person's confession with forgiveness. Some people have twisted confession into meaning indiscriminate, public, and sometimes humiliating blurtings out of sin. Donald W. Burdick sets us straight on this matter.

> If a person has sinned against a brother, he should confess the sin to him. This will no doubt result in mutual confession—"to each other." Then the two believers should "pray for each other." If the sin has caused sickness, healing will follow confession and prayer. James proceeds to add the assurance that prayer "is powerful and effective." The "righteous man" here referred to is the man whose sins have been confessed and forgiven.[8]

Concluding Principles

In summary, here are five lingering principles to tuck into your memory.

- *The will of God is paramount. Respect it.* Remember, our God can do whatever He pleases with whomever He chooses whenever He wishes.

- *The use of medical assistance is imperative. Seek it and obey it.* Don't ignore God's provision of doctors' knowledge and available medicines. Instead, gratefully use it, all the while committing yourself to prayer.

- *Confession of sin is healthy. Employ it appropriately and honestly.* Deal truthfully with your sins, but remember not to be indiscriminate in sharing them. It's usually best to go privately to the people whom you've directly sinned against.

- *Praying for one another is commanded. Practice it.* All of us are sinners who need each other's prayerful encouragement and support.

8. Donald W. Burdick, "James," in *The Expositor's Bible Commentary*, gen. ed. Frank E. Gaebelein (Grand Rapids, Mich.: Zondervan Publishing House, Regency Reference Library, 1981), vol. 12, p. 204.

- *When healing comes from God, gratefully accept it.* Sing His praises, as James says (v. 13). Remember to thank God and give Him the glory.

We won't escape the ravages of sin, sickness, and suffering in this world. But a new world is coming where everything will be set right (Rev. 21:1–7)! In the meantime, let's trust the Lord to know what's best for us and rely on the comfort of His always being with us, "even to the end of the age" (Matt. 28:20).

Living Insights

Are you struggling with major or prolonged sickness? Have you followed James' prescription: (1) make others aware of your needs, (2) seek medical attention, and (3) ask the elders of your church to pray over you? If you've overlooked any of James' counsel, what do you need to do?

_____

_____

Could personal sin be the cause of some of your physical problems? Has anger or jealousy caused you sleepless nights, headaches, or ulcers? To help diagnose your condition, set aside some time to pray through David's words in Psalm 139:23–24, and search your heart for any "hurtful way" that needs to be confessed.

_____

_____

_____

_____

_____

For those of you in the merciless hands of an unrelenting illness, please know that we are not assuming personal sin is the root of all suffering. As we saw clearly in our lesson, sin and sickness are not always linked. Rather, God may be using our physical sufferings to display His works in us (John 9:1–3). What do you think God might be displaying, or wants to display, through your sickness or affliction?

_____

_____

_____

_____

_____

If you're having trouble understanding God's work in your life, let Paul show you what he discovered:

> There was given me a thorn in the flesh. . . . Concerning this I implored the Lord three times that it might leave me. And He has said to me, "My grace is sufficient for you, for power is perfected in weakness." (2 Cor. 12:7b, 8–9a)

May God grant that you will see His grace and power revealed through your weakness.

Chapter 11

THE GATHERING STORM AROUND JESUS

Selected Scriptures

So far in our study, we have seen Jesus

generously offer abundant life,
graciously provide rest for weary souls,
tenderly heal the sick, the lame, the blind,
compassionately feed the hungry and needy,
and miraculously bring the dead back to life.

How is it, then, that someone so kind and giving ended His life hammered to a cross? Why would anyone hate Jesus so much that they'd want to kill Him?

Because He was a threat.

He was more than "gentle Jesus, meek and mild." He actively opposed the evil in the world . . . and the evil within each human heart. Jesus Himself explained,

> "The Light has come into the world, and men loved the darkness rather than the Light, for their deeds were evil. For everyone who does evil hates the Light, and does not come to the Light for fear that his deeds will be exposed. . . . The world . . . hates Me because I testify of it, that its deeds are evil." (John 3:19–20; 7:7)

We like light that shows us to our best advantage—flattering our better side, keeping our flaws hidden, softening our wrinkles and the hardness in our eyes. Jesus' light, however, goes beyond our outward attempts at beauty to reveal what's inside—a terminal disease called sin and its by-products of loneliness, fear, and pain. He shows us where we are in relation to where God wants us to be.

Is He trying to humiliate us—leave us naked and ashamed under a harsh, merciless glare? Not at all. He wants to bring healing to what He reveals, to bring change that takes us from death to life.

The trouble is, we don't always see our need of healing. We

don't always want to see our need for change. Tragically, our human pride prefers "a way that seems right . . . but its end is the way of death" (Prov. 14:12).

Which is how the Life, who was the Light of the World, wound up crucified.

Jesus: Prince of Peace . . . and Conflict

In Matthew's Gospel, Jesus makes a startling—even audacious—statement about His ministry:

> "Do not think that I came to bring peace on the earth; I did not come to bring peace, but a sword. For I came to set a man against his father, and a daughter against her mother, and a daughter-in-law against her mother-in-law; and a man's enemies will be the members of his household." (Matt. 10:34–36)

Wow! How does this jibe with the angels' words at Jesus' birth: "I bring you good news of great joy which will be for all the people. . . . Glory to God in the highest, And on earth *peace* . . ." (Luke 2:10, 14, emphasis added)? Commentator D. A. Carson helps us put this together.

> As many Jews in Jesus' day thought the coming of Messiah would bring them political peace and material prosperity, so today many in the church think that Jesus' presence will bring them a kind of tranquility. But Jesus insisted that his mission entailed strife and division (v. 34). Prince of Peace though he is . . . the world will so violently reject him and his reign that men and women will divide over him (vv. 35–36). . . . Before the consummation of the kingdom, even the peace Jesus bequeaths his disciples will have its setting in the midst of a hostile world (John 14:27; 16:33; cf. James 4:4).[1]

1. D. A. Carson, "Matthew," in *The Expositor's Bible Commentary*, gen. ed. Frank E. Gaebelein (Grand Rapids, Mich.: Zondervan Publishing House, Regency Reference Library, 1984), vol. 8, pp. 256–57. Jesus quotes from Micah 7:6, where, Carson explains, the prophet "describes the sinfulness and rebellion in the days of King Ahaz; but insofar as Jesus' disciples by following him align themselves with the prophets ([Matt.] 5:10–12), then the situation in Micah's time points to the greater division at Messiah's coming" (p. 257).

Remember, the angels didn't announce worldwide peace but "peace among men with whom He is pleased" (Luke 2:14b). And God was not pleased with the hypocrisy, greed, and corruption of those who should have been leading His people in the way of truth: the religious leaders of Jesus' day.

Clashes with the Pharisees, Sadducees, Scribes, and Priests

As Jesus' ministry gained momentum, His opposition did too. When He healed the sick and freed those possessed by demons, the Pharisees and scribes criticized Him for performing miracles on the Sabbath and attributed His power over demons to the demons! They excommunicated any Jew who dared to believe and follow Jesus. Their rage quickly escalated to plots to have Jesus arrested and killed. You can trace the religious leaders' hatred throughout each of the Gospel accounts with the following references:

Matthew	Mark	Luke	John
9:34; 12:10, 14, 24; 15:12; 21:45–46; 22:15; 26:3–5	3:2, 6, 22; 11:18; 12:12; 14:1–2	6:11; 11:15, 53–54; 13:17; 16:14; 19:47–48; 20:19–20	5:16, 18; 6:41; 7:25, 32; 8:48, 52, 59; 9:22; 10:31, 39; 11:53, 57; 12:10, 42

Let's look at a few of these scenes more in-depth to see just what Jesus was doing that made these men so murderously angry.

He Stood against Man-Made Religion

From headquarters in Jerusalem, a delegation of Pharisees and scribes came all the way to the Galilee region to confront Jesus.

> "Why do Your disciples break the tradition of the elders? For they do not wash their hands when they eat bread." (Matt. 15:2)

They traveled these many miles because the disciples didn't wash up before supper? Well, it's a little more complex than that.

> The Pharisees were scrupulous about washing their hands as part of ritual purity, though this rule was not found in the Old Testament. . . . Washing the hands removed partial ceremonial impurity picked up in the marketplace; hands were apparently immersed up to the wrist or purified by having water

84

poured over them from a pure vessel. The Pharisees also had rules about immersing vessels to remove impurity.[2]

So it wasn't just good hygiene but spiritual purity that was at stake. Jesus quickly set them straight about the true nature of spirituality.

> "Why do you yourselves transgress the commandment of God for the sake of your tradition? For God said, 'Honor your father and mother,' and, 'He who speaks evil of father or mother is to be put to death.' But you say, 'Whoever says to his father or mother, "Whatever I have that would help you has been given to God," he is not to honor his father or his mother.' And by this you invalidated the word of God for the sake of your tradition." (vv. 3–6)

Jesus stripped their man-made traditions of any authority and focused on the commandments that did need to be observed—God's commandments. You see, over time hundreds of interpretations, comments, rules, and regulations had been added to the Law that Moses gave the people. The Pharisees and scribes regarded them as equal with the canon of Scripture. To them, it was just as important to obey their traditions as it was to obey God's commandments.

Jesus, however, exposed the corruption in their tradition. Their rules allowed a man to not honor his mother and father—God's own command—by keeping "his property out of his parents' reach by nominally dedicating it to God (while in practice retaining the use of it for himself)."[3] And Jesus wasn't going to stand for it.

> "You hypocrites, rightly did Isaiah prophesy of you:
> 'This people honors Me with their lips,
> But their heart is far away from Me.
> But in vain do they worship Me,
> Teaching as doctrines the precepts of men.'"
> (vv. 7–9)

2. Craig S. Keener, *The IVP Bible Background Commentary: New Testament* (Downers Grove, Ill.: InterVarsity Press, 1993), pp. 152–53.

3. Richard T. France, "Matthew," in the *New Bible Commentary: 21st Century Edition*, ed. D. A. Carson, R. T. France, J. A. Motyer, and G. J. Wenham (Downers Grove, Ill.: InterVarsity Press, 1994), p. 924.

His disciples' reaction? "Do You know that the Pharisees were offended . . . ?" (v. 12). Now there's an understatement! Of course He knew, because when Jesus encountered wrong, when He came to the place where compromise would encourage opposition to the Word of God, He boldly called it what it was.

Nowhere was His boldness so unsparing and sustained as in Matthew 23, where He lambastes the scribes and Pharisees for putting up barriers that blocked the people's way to God.

He Stood against Hypocrisy

Seven times in Matthew 23, like seven stinging slaps in the face, Jesus denounced the scribes and Pharisees and called them what they were: "Woe to you, scribes and Pharisees, hypocrites!" (vv. 13, 14, 15, 23, 25, 27, 29). He also threw in "blind guides," "fools," "serpents," and "brood of vipers" for good measure. This is not the way you win friends and influence people. But it is the way Jesus unchained the truth so it, in turn, could set people free.

This chapter, Richard T. France tells us,

> shows Jesus as a fierce controversialist, quite willing to make enemies when the cause demanded it. And the cause was important, for what was at issue was the contrast between the values of the kingdom of heaven and the superficial approach to religion which has already been unmasked especially in 5:17–48 and 15:1–20.[4]

Here's a catalogue of what the Pharisees and scribes had accomplished with their "superficial approach to religion":

- They laid heavy burdens on people's shoulders with their rules and regulations, but they would not lift even a finger to help them (23:4).

- They sought the spotlight with their religious observances, not God's heart (vv. 5–7).

- They wouldn't go in and they wouldn't let others enter the kingdom of heaven (v. 13).

- They took advantage of the most vulnerable and covered their wickedness with a show of religion (v. 14).

4. France, "Matthew," p. 934.

- They made converts who out-Phariseed even the Pharisees, legalistic to the core and without room for Jesus the Messiah (v. 15).

- They created a system of oath-making that destroyed the truth (vv. 16–22).

- They gave so much attention to the little details of the law that they missed the more important matters of justice, mercy, and faithfulness (vv. 23–24).

- They focused on outer cleanliness but neglected to deal with the filth of their souls (vv. 25–28).

- They claimed superiority over their ancestors who murdered the prophets, yet they themselves had been plotting to kill Jesus (vv. 29–36).

And Jesus was not done with them yet.

He Stood against Greed

When Jesus came to Jerusalem, He headed for His Father's house —the temple. What did He find there? A flea market![5] Merchants hawked priest-certified animals for Passover sacrifice, and money-changers sat behind tables milking foreign visitors with their exorbitant exchange rates. Instead of whispered prayers, Jesus heard clinking coins. Instead of incense, He smelled the dung of sheep and cattle.

Who was behind this exploitative monopoly? William Barclay writes that "these Temple shops were known as the Booths of Annas and were the property of the family of the High Priest."[6] Rather than praying for the people, these hypocritical priests were preying on the people. Jesus exploded at them:

> Jesus entered the temple and began to drive out those who were selling, saying to them, "It is written, 'And My house shall be a house of prayer,' but you have made it a robbers' den." (Luke 19:45–46)

5. This section has been adapted from the study guide *The Consummation of Something Miraculous: A Study of Luke 16:19–24:53*, coauthored by Bryce Klabunde, from the Bible-teaching ministry of Charles R. Swindoll (Anaheim, Calif.: Insight for Living, 1995), pp. 63–64.

6. William Barclay, *The Gospel of Luke*, rev. ed., The Daily Study Bible Series (Philadelphia, Pa.: Westminster Press, 1975), p. 242.

John tells us that Jesus "made a scourge of cords," which He used to whip the profane merchants as He overturned their tables (John 2:15). This is a picture of a righteously indignant Jesus, and it didn't endear Him to the corrupt religious leaders:

> And He was teaching daily in the temple; but the chief priests and the scribes and the leading men among the people were trying to destroy Him, and they could not find anything that they might do, for all the people were hanging on to every word He said. (Luke 19:47–48)

We need to realize that when we follow Jesus, we're following someone dangerous. Someone who overthrows the status quo. Someone who speaks out against evil. Someone who tells the truth, no matter the personal cost. Do we? Do we speak up for the poor, for the oppressed, for the abused, for the helpless? Do we speak against the distortion of who God is, against lies, racism, prejudice, exploitation, violence, injustice? Or do we stay in the background, letting evil run its course so we can continue to enjoy our food and shelter and all the comfortable things in life?

We don't need to become wild-eyed zealots, but far too many of us are far too passive. Remember the words of the Lord recorded by Ezekiel:

> "Behold, this was the guilt of your sister Sodom: she and her daughters had arrogance, abundant food and careless ease, but she did not help the poor and needy." (Ezek. 16:49)

Four Concluding Applications

As imitators of Christ, how do we bring these scenes from His life into our lives? Here are four suggestions.

First, *remembering our mission helps us navigate through the storm.* Jesus was the Way, the Truth, and the Life, and He came not "to be served, but to serve, and to give His life a ransom for many" (Mark 10:45). His mission was redemption, and we share in that mission when we point people to Him. We are called to reflect Him, in all His love, kindness, forgiveness, and grace—and also in His truth. So when a storm of opposition hits, let's remember what God has called us to and stay focused.

Second, *encountering evil often requires sword-like confrontation.*

Jesus didn't soften His message or compromise with the Pharisees to avoid a confrontation. Rather, He called their actions what they were because God's honor and people's eternal lives were at stake. Now, we're not omnipotent, like He is, but we still have a responsibility to remain alert, stand up for what's right, and stand against what's wrong. How many people remained silent to the plight of slaves in this country? How many in Europe looked the other way when Nazi soldiers dragged their Jewish neighbors out of their homes in the middle of the night and crammed them into cattle cars? At the least, we have a responsibility to warn others when they're going astray, as the Lord communicated when He commissioned Ezekiel as Israel's watchman:

> "When I say to the wicked, 'You will surely die,' and you do not warn him or speak out to warn the wicked from his wicked way that he may live, that wicked man shall die in his iniquity, but his blood I will require at your hand." (Ezek. 3:18)

Third, *being bold when there's a principle worth fighting for is worth the risk.* "Take these things away," Jesus ordered the sellers of doves at the temple, "Stop making My Father's house a place of business" (John 2:16). Preserving the purity of worship is worth fighting for, and so is preserving the purity of the gospel. Our opinions and traditions, on the other hand, are probably not eternal principles, so we need to evaluate our causes carefully. Remember, being courageous for what matters to God glorifies Him, but being just plain feisty, or as Paul put it in 1 Timothy 3:3, "pugnacious," does not.

Fourth, *speaking up for what is right is no guarantee you'll win or be respected.* Jesus wound up on a cross, remember? "If they persecuted Me, they will also persecute you," Jesus warned His disciples (John 15:20). "If the world hates you, you know that it has hated me before it hated you" (v. 18). Life is not like a Hollywood movie, where Mr. Smith goes to Washington, stands against political corruption, gets knocked to the ground, but is ultimately vindicated. It's all too often like Archbishop Oscar Romero, who spoke against the injustice that oppressed the people of El Salvador and was assassinated in the middle of leading a church service. We do right because it is God's way, and that will keep us realistic in our expectations.

Yes, Jesus wound up on a cross. But He also walked out of a tomb and ascended into heaven to be seated at the right hand of the Father. He defeated sin and death, and when He comes again in glory, He will be the victor, not the vanquished ever again. And He has good news for us too:

> "Do not let your heart be troubled; believe in God, believe also in Me. In My Father's house are many dwelling places; if it were not so, I would have told you; for I go to prepare a place for you. If I go and prepare a place for you, I will come again and receive you to Myself, that where I am, there you may be also." (John 14:1–3)

Living Insights

It's easy for us to identify with Jesus—it's certainly a lot more comfortable! But it may be more honest to admit that we have some Pharisee in us as well. Let's spend a little time allowing Christ's Spirit to reveal any areas of darkness in us that need the light of His healing.

Do you have traditions, perhaps in your church or in your family, that have taken on equal importance with God's way? These could be legalistic restrictions—no makeup, no movies, no dancing. They could be prejudices, such as no dating people of other nationalities. Is there anything like this in your life? If so, bring them into the light by naming them.

_____

_____

_____

How do Jesus' words in Matthew 15:3–9 apply to you, if they do? What solution do they present?

_____

_____

_____

_____

Reread Matthew 23 and the bulleted list that summarized it in our chapter. Does any of Jesus' exposé apply to you? How?

_____

_____

_____

If blindness and hypocrisy lurk in the shadows of your life, don't be afraid to bring them to Christ. Read what He said in verse 37. If you're willing, He wants to gather you protectively in His arms, like "a hen gathers her chicks under her wings," rescuing you from your sin. Are you willing to come to Him? Write down what He reveals that needs to change in you.

_____

_____

_____

_____

Has the love of making money become more central for you than loving and worshiping God? Does Jesus need to overturn something in your life? If so, what is it? How do His words in Matthew 6:24 relate to you?

_____

_____

_____

If this is a dark area for you, Jesus offers His light in Matthew 6:19–21. What kind of changes can these verses begin to make in your life?

_____

_____

_____

Remember, Jesus' light is not the enemy; the darkness is. And Jesus' purpose is not to shame or humiliate us but rather to call us "out of darkness into His marvelous light," where we receive His mercy and become His very own chosen people (1 Pet. 2:8–10).

Chapter 12

BETRAYED AND ARRESTED

Selected Scriptures

The storm gathering around Jesus grew continually more ominous. With the persistence of stalking lions, the Jewish officials watched and waited for a way to entrap Jesus and put Him to death.

Thankfully, Jesus still had His faithful followers, His circle of friends. None of them would ever turn against Him, especially not one of the Twelve—His chosen few—right? Wrong.

Because there was Judas. His name in Hebrew once meant "praised"; now it forever hisses with betrayal. Who was this man, and how did he come to be the most infamous traitor? Let's look at the clues the Gospel writers give us to see why he took such a treacherous turn.

One of Jesus' Chosen

Jesus had many disciples (John 6:66–67), but He handpicked only twelve, with Judas being among these select few:

> Simon, whom He also named Peter, and Andrew his brother; and James and John; and Philip and Bartholomew; and Matthew and Thomas; James the son of Alphaeus, and Simon who was called the Zealot; Judas the son of James, and Judas Iscariot, who became a traitor. (Luke 6:14–16)

As an apostle (v. 13), Judas ministered shoulder to shoulder with Jesus and the others who were specially chosen.

> Jesus summoned His twelve disciples and gave them authority over unclean spirits, to cast them out, and to heal every kind of disease and every kind of sickness. (Matt. 10:1; see also vv. 5–8)

What a privilege! Each disciple must have felt a sense of awe for being given the chance to participate with Jesus in changing the world. Not only that, but each of them, including Judas, received personal and intimate instruction from Jesus for three years. Many times the Gospels tell us that Jesus retreated into isolation with His disciples and that He took them aside to teach or reveal secrets to them. He gave them more of His time than He gave any other people on earth, including His own family. In addition, Jesus singled out Judas for the trusted responsibility of handling the money for Him (John 13:29).

Despite all these privileges, however, Judas turned traitor. Why did he change? What happened in his heart? How did he go from an apostle to an apostate?

One Who Chose to Betray

Judas' betrayal fulfilled prophecy (Ps. 41:9), but was he merely a robot, programmed to mindlessly obey God's divinely appointed plan? No, Judas had a free will, and he chose willingly to act as he did. Let's comb through the Gospels now to uncover what may have led to his downward spiral.

Disillusioned

Judas' full name, Judas Iscariot, is our first clue. Iscariot may indicate one of four things:

- that Judas came from the town Kerioth, which may have been in Judah;

- that his name may have been derived from the Aramaic word for *lie*, making him the "man of the lie," which would classify him as a traitor;

- that Iscariot means "dyer," indicating that he dyed cloth as his profession;

- that Iscariot comes from the word *sicarius,* meaning "dagger bearer" or "assassin."[1]

The last possibility may be the most probable. George Wesley Buchanan tells us that "in Palestine, during the lifetime of Jesus, the *sicarii* were extremely zealous Jewish nationalists, who carried daggers under their cloaks so that they could take advantage of every opportunity to kill Romans or Roman collaborators."[2] Their

---

1. George Wesley Buchanan, "Judas Iscariot," in *The International Standard Bible Encyclopedia,* rev. ed., gen. ed. Geoffrey W. Bromiley (1982; reprint, Grand Rapids, Mich.: William B. Eerdmans Publishing Co., 1987), vol. 2, pp. 1151–52.

2. Buchanan, "Judas Iscariot," p. 1152.

hope was for a messiah who would be a political revolutionary, delivering them from Roman oppression and restoring a kingdom of peace, justice, and abundance to Israel (see Acts 1:6). This, however, was not who Jesus would be.

After Jesus miraculously fed the five thousand (John 6:1–13), the people's excitement grew. They said, "This is truly the Prophet who is to come into the world" (v. 14; see also Deut. 18:15–18). Judas must have thought, *Wow! Now is the time for Jesus to act. He's got to take advantage of this opportunity and gather the people to move against Rome.* But Jesus disappointed His zealous followers:

> So Jesus, perceiving that they were intending to come and take Him by force to make Him king, withdrew again to the mountain by Himself alone. (John 6:15)

This was not the way to be king, according to Judas' plan. Nor was Jesus' discourse about being the Bread of Life (vv. 26–58). "Unless you eat the flesh of the Son of Man and drink His blood," Jesus told the crowd, "you have no life in yourselves" (v. 53). Rather than increasing His numbers, He was thinning the ranks: "As a result of this many of His disciples withdrew and were not walking with Him anymore" (v. 66).

Judas didn't understand what Jesus was doing, and he most likely felt his dreams for an earthly kingdom slipping away. Maybe this Man on whom he had pinned all his hopes was just some religious fanatic, befriending the poor and powerless and antagonizing the religious establishment. Judas didn't want to serve; he wanted to rule. With his dreams dashed, disillusionment set in, and a cynical bitterness soon followed.

Jesus recognized what was happening long before Judas fully did. After the crowds dwindled, Jesus told the Twelve who remained by His side, "Did I Myself not choose you, the twelve, and yet one of you is a devil?" (v. 70). And the devil's ways would soon show in Judas' life.

Defrauding

While staying with Martha, Mary, and Lazarus, whom Jesus had just raised from the dead, Jesus was anointed for His own approaching death and burial.

Mary then took a pound of very costly perfume of

pure nard,[3] and anointed the feet of Jesus and wiped His feet with her hair; and the house was filled with the fragrance of the perfume. (12:3)

The sweet smell that filled the house burned like sulfur in Judas' nostrils. All the disciples were offended (see Matt. 26:8; Mark 14:4), yet only Judas, the protector of the money box, spoke out against this lavish "waste": "Why was this perfume not sold for three hundred denarii and given to poor people?" (John 12:5). How charitable and frugal . . . and false:

> Now he said this, not because he was concerned about the poor, but because he was a thief, and as he had the money box, he used to pilfer what was put into it. (v. 6)

William Barclay gives us this insight into Judas' character, and our own:

> Judas had just seen an action of surpassing loveliness; and he called it extravagant waste. He was an embittered man and he took an embittered view of things. . . . A warped mind brings a warped view of things; and, if we find ourselves becoming very critical of others and imputing unworthy motives to them, we should, for a moment, stop examining them and start examining ourselves.[4]

Jesus, knowing His disciple's heart and Mary's, did not let Judas' remark go by. "Let her alone," He said (v. 7), or in our language, "Back off." She was tenderly and reverently preparing Jesus' body for burial—His death was so near. "You always have the poor with you," Jesus reminded Judas, "but you do not always have Me" (v. 8). Clearly, Judas was in it for what he could get out of it, but Jesus was in it for what He could give away.

Scripture doesn't record Judas' response to Jesus' rebuke, but it's easy to imagine from what he did next that his initial embarrassment quickly turned to rage.

---

3. Judas estimates the value of this perfume at three hundred denarii—almost a year's wages.

4. William Barclay, *The Gospel of John*, vol. 2, rev. ed., The Daily Study Bible Series (Philadelphia, Pa.: Westminster Press, 1975), p. 112.

Judas' growing hatred for Jesus opened the door for a sinister presence.

> Now the Feast of Unleavened Bread, which is called the Passover, was approaching. The chief priests and the scribes were seeking how they might put Him to death; for they were afraid of the people.
>
> And Satan entered into Judas who was called Iscariot, belonging to the number of the twelve. And he went away and discussed with the chief priests and officers how he might betray Him to them. They were glad and agreed to give him money. So he consented, and began seeking a good opportunity to betray Him to them apart from the crowd. (Luke 22:1–6)

"Satan entered into Judas"—we ought to shudder at this statement. This is not merely one of Satan's demons possessing and terrifying a person, which is horrible enough; it is the Evil One himself. We don't know the details of how this happened, but as commentator Darrell Bock explains, "The subsequent events occur because Satan has his way with Judas. . . . When Satan enters a life, he leads the person in sinister directions."[5]

Satan is the father of lies (John 8:44), and Judas lived a gross deception. John tells us that at the Last Supper with His disciples, after washing their feet—even Judas'—Jesus honored Judas by giving him the seat next to Himself at the table and offering him the dipped morsel (13:26). Outwardly, Judas looked like the others, but inside he was following Satan's orders (vv. 27, 30). Jesus was offering him one last chance, but Judas stubbornly refused to take it, as Bruce Milne points out:

> For one last, lingering moment Judas' destiny hangs in the balance as the love of God incarnate shines one more time into his benighted heart. But the moment is no sooner present than it passes, as Judas in a final act of defiance closes his heart against the light, and turns away into the darkness that has no end.[6]

5. Darrell L. Bock, *Luke*, The IVP New Testament Commentary Series (Downers Grove, Ill.: InterVarsity Press, 1994), p. 346.

6. Bruce Milne, *The Message of John: Here Is Your King!*, The Bible Speaks Today Series (Downers Grove, Ill.: InterVarsity Press, 1993), pp. 202–3.

A few hours later, Judas, along with a mob armed with clubs and swords, approached Jesus in the Garden of Gethsemane. Telling the chief priests and elders, "Whomever I kiss, He is the one; seize Him" (Matt. 26:48), Judas then turned a gesture of love and affection into an everlasting picture of treachery (v. 49). True to the plan, Jesus' enemies seized Him, arrested Him, and moved swiftly to crucify Him.

Satan, finished with his pawn, left Judas to face what he had done—alone, so terribly, finally alone.

Despairing

"No matter what the devil promises," Darrell Bock reminds us, "Satan's entry into one's life is destructive."[7] Having rejected the Light of the World and having followed in the steps of the Prince of Darkness, Judas had nowhere to turn when the truth of his actions hit him. His last resort was to go to his coconspirators and try to stop this terrible injustice.

> When Judas, who had betrayed Him, saw that He had been condemned, he felt remorse and returned the thirty pieces of silver to the chief priests and elders, saying, "I have sinned by betraying innocent blood." But they said, "What is that to us? See to that yourself!" And he threw the pieces of silver into the temple sanctuary and departed; and he went away and hanged himself. (27:3–5)

Poor Judas. The former tool of Satan found the Evil One hard at work in the hearts of the priests of God. The thieving lover of money couldn't get rid of his blood wages fast enough. The deceitful betrayer of the Word of Life took his own life . . . apart from friends, apart from family, apart from God.

Choosing to Learn and Live

What can we learn from Judas' tragic life? Four lingering lessons come to mind.

First, *association with the godly is no guarantee of godliness*. Three years with God's own Son made no impact for godliness on Judas. A

---

7. Bock, *Luke*, p. 346.

lifetime of church attendance won't guarantee our godliness either. The work of holiness is done in the heart.

Second, *wickedness in secret is as wrong as wickedness in public.* If we see wickedness, we can protect ourselves against it (Prov. 27:12). But if it is concealed, subtle, and devious, we are so much more vulnerable. Satan himself had infiltrated Judas' life, and the other disciples didn't even know it (John 13:29).

Third, *Satan and his demons are willing to work with anyone who desires to work against God.* In some churches, Satan is the most active member. He prowls for anyone—the trusted, the pious, the admired—whom he can use to tear apart the body of Christ. We should take care not to allow division or conflict to give Satan any kind of foothold.

Fourth, *no sorrow can compare to the remorse of those who discover too late that they're on the wrong side.* Judas had set the wheels of cruel injustice turning, and he was powerless to stop them. No prayer accompanying his regret was recorded, just his desperate realization. Nothing can compare to the sorrow felt over a wrongdoing that can't be undone.

Jesus Christ may offer a narrow way, a life of service, and a cross to bear, but He also promises eternal life, peace, joy, hope, comfort, and love. Satan offers power, ease, and pleasure today, but the tomorrow he brings is one of degradation, despair, and destruction. "I have set before you life and death, the blessing and the curse," God tells us, "so choose life in order that you may live" (Deut. 30:19).

Living Insights

Many people, Christians included, get involved in satanic activities, sometimes without even realizing it.[8] For example, do you know someone who reads their horoscope—just for kicks? Someone who visits the palm reader at the county fair or plays with a Ouija board or tarot cards? All of these are in the realm of the occult, areas of darkness.

Take a look at how specific God's commands are concerning occult involvement, and jot down what you find.

---

8. This Living Insight has been adapted from the study guide *The Life and Times of Elijah*, coauthored by David Lien, from the Bible-teaching ministry of Charles R. Swindoll (Anaheim, Calif.: Insight for Living, 1992), pp. 79–80.

Deuteronomy 18:9–13 _____

_____

_____

_____

Isaiah 8:19–22 _____

_____

_____

_____

Isaiah 47:9–15_____

_____

_____

_____

Galatians 5:19–20 _____

_____

_____

_____

Have you allowed the occult to make even the smallest inroad in your life? These activities may seem fun and harmless, but harmless and powerless they are not. To remain unaware of that truth is to leave yourself frighteningly unprotected against Satan's deadly games. Write down and bring into the light any areas of darkness you are playing with.

_____

_____

_____

_____

How has your involvement affected you or others?

_____

_____

_____

_____

Do you fully realize who is behind these activities? Read John 8:44, 1 Peter 5:8, and Revelation 12:10, and write down his true identity.

_____

_____

_____

When Satan entered Judas at the Last Supper, and the disciple left to betray his Lord, John makes this simple, arresting statement, "And it was night" (John 13:30). William Barclay makes these observations that we would do well to consider.

> It was night for the day was late; but there was another night there. It is always night when a man goes from Christ to follow his own purposes. It is always night when a man listens to the call of evil rather than the summons of good. It is always night when hate puts out the light of love. It is always night when a man turns his back on Jesus. . . . The way of light and the way of dark are set before us. . . . In the dark a man always goes lost.[9]

9. Barclay, *The Gospel of John*, vol. 2, p. 147.

Chapter 13

ANALYSIS OF A COURTROOM FIASCO

Selected Scriptures

For three and a half years, Jesus watched as a band of Jewish leaders grew in their hostility toward Him. With cunning and ruthlessness, an unholy alliance of Pharisees, Sadducees, scribes, and priests plotted His demise.

These vengeful men staged the final scenes of their plan with meticulous care. Having contracted the help of the insider Judas, they orchestrated Jesus' arrest and set their scheme in motion.

At the appointed time—nighttime, when no crowds would be present—Judas led the officials to Jesus. The Lord had just finished praying in the Garden of Gethsemane, a secluded spot, a place Judas knew well since Jesus had taken His disciples there many times. Judas identified Jesus with a kiss of betrayal, and then allowed the soldiers to do the rest.[1]

The clanking of armor and spears rattled against the hush of the dark air. Quivering tongues of orange flame licked the black night, and soon the grove found itself crowded with stone-faced soldiers and salivating betrayers who could think only of quenching their bloodlust.

Betrayal and Arrest in the Garden

Before the soldiers could go for their swords, Jesus took the initiative.

This chapter has been adapted from "Arrest and Trial" and "Rush to Judgment," in the study guide *Beholding Christ . . . The Lamb of God: A Study of John 15–21,* coauthored by Ken Gire, from the Bible-teaching ministry of Charles R. Swindoll (Fullerton, Calif.: Insight for Living, 1987); and "A Closer Look at Jesus' Arrest and Trials," in the study guide *A Look at the Book: Traveling the Original Route Sixty-Six,* coauthored by Lee Hough and Bryce Klabunde, from the Bible-teaching ministry of Charles R. Swindoll (Anaheim, Calif.: Insight for Living, 1994).

1. A "cohort" of soldiers, *speira* in Greek, numbered two hundred to a thousand men and was commanded by a *chiliarchos* or "commander" (see v. 12). See D. A. Carson, *The Gospel according to John* (Grand Rapids, Mich.: William B. Eerdmans Publishing Co., 1991), p. 577. The large number of soldiers not only ensured the success of the arrest but also would have staved off any fight that might have arisen.

So Jesus, knowing all the things that were coming upon Him, went forth and said to them, "Whom do you seek?" They answered Him, "Jesus the Nazarene." He said to them, "I am He." And Judas also, who was betraying Him, was standing with them. So when He said to them, "I am He," they drew back and fell to the ground. Therefore He again asked them, "Whom do you seek?" And they said, "Jesus the Nazarene." Jesus answered, "I told you that I am He; so if you seek Me, let these go their way," to fulfill the word which He spoke, "Of those whom You have given Me I lost not one." (John 18:4–9)

Like a lamb silent before its shearers, Jesus offered no resistance.[2] Not so with Peter, who decided to do a little shearing of his own.

Simon Peter then, having a sword, drew it and struck the high priest's slave, and cut off his right ear; and the slave's name was Malchus. (v. 10)

Jesus, however, reminded Peter that violence was the world's way, not God's way.

So Jesus said to Peter, "Put the sword into the sheath; the cup which the Father has given Me, shall I not drink it?" (v. 11)

Jesus then mercifully healed the man's ear (Luke 22:51). This, too, was lost on the Jewish officials, who were pleased that they would finally be able to accomplish their mission.

So the Roman cohort and the commander and the officers of the Jews, arrested Jesus and bound Him. (John 18:12)

Arrested and bound. John describes the event so matter-of-factly, yet it probably involved humiliation and violence. Rome's police force was its army, and the soldiers—much like the police of today—faced dangerous criminals daily. These men were not likely given to gentleness or kind words on the job. Their binding of Jesus probably involved twisting His wrists behind His back and knocking Him to the ground.

---

2. This fulfilled the prophecy in Isaiah 53:7.

From this point on, Jesus would no longer be a free man. He became the property of the state, railroaded through the most fallacious, unfair, disorderly, illegal series of trials in the history of jurisprudence. No trial could have been more unjust.

Between 2 A.M. and 7:30 A.M., Jesus would be subjected to not one but six trials—three Jewish and three Roman (summarized in the chart at the end of this chapter). The charge in the Jewish proceedings would be blasphemy; but because the Jews were not allowed to administer capital punishment, they would change the charge to treason, which, in Rome, was punishable by crucifixion.

The Jewish Trials

The Jews were not without laws that safeguarded justice in legal proceedings. But you wouldn't have known it looking at the account of Jesus' first three trials. William Barclay notes the specific trial laws they broke in His case:

> All criminal cases must be tried during the daytime and must be completed during the daytime. Criminal cases could not be transacted during the Passover season at all. Only if the verdict was Not Guilty could a case be finished on the day it was begun; otherwise a night must elapse before the pronouncement of the verdict, so that feelings of mercy might have time to arise. . . . All evidence had to be guaranteed by two witnesses separately examined and having no contact with each other. And false witness was punishable by death.[3]

The Jews, however, broke a legion of their own laws to convict and crucify an innocent man.

Trial 1: Before Annas

Jesus' first illegal trial took place during the hours of darkness at the house of Annas. Annas, the father-in-law of Caiaphas the high priest, was the wealthiest and most influential man in the city. He owned and operated the entire money-changing system, which was corrupt to the core and behind the group Jesus chased from the

---

3. William Barclay, *The Gospel of Matthew*, vol. 2, rev. ed., The Daily Study Bible Series (Philadelphia, Pa.: Westminster Press, 1975), p. 353.

temple. He had served as the high priest for nine years and was now sort of a high priest emeritus. He was the power behind the throne in Jewry, and ever since Jesus upset his business in the temple courtyard, Annas most likely had a personal vendetta against Him.[4]

So, with Jesus fettered in chains before him, Annas gloatingly interrogated Him on two counts: His teaching and His disciples (John 18:19). Jesus answered with no excuses:

> "I have spoken openly to the world; I always taught in synagogues and in the temple, where all the Jews come together; and I spoke nothing in secret. Why do you question Me? Question those who have heard what I spoke to them; they know what I said." (vv. 20–21)

Jesus' unflinching response placed the burden of proof where it belonged—squarely on the shoulders of His accuser. The reaction from the impartial and fair court?

> When He had said this, one of the officers standing nearby struck Jesus, saying, "Is that the way You answer the high priest?" (v. 22)

Jesus, however, remained steadfast.

> "If I have spoken wrongly, testify of the wrong; but if rightly, why do you strike Me?" (v. 23)

Nowhere does Scripture record an answer to Jesus' question. All we know is that "Annas sent Him bound to Caiaphas the high priest" (v. 24). Their scheme was now in full stride, and no challenges by the Savior—no matter how unjust He revealed their behavior to be—were going to stop them now.

Trial 2: Before Caiaphas

Caiaphas was a pawn in Rome and equally as corrupt as Annas. Jesus was brought still bound to his home in the middle of the night—an illegality that didn't seem to bother this high priest at all. As the ruling member of the Sanhedrin, he was responsible for ensuring a fair trial, but justice was not his concern with Jesus.

---

4. William Barclay, *The Gospel of John*, vol. 2, rev. ed., The Daily Study Bible Series (Philadelphia, Pa.: Westminster Press, 1975), pp. 225–27.

> They led Jesus away to the high priest; and all
> the chief priests and the elders and the scribes gath-
> ered together. . . . Now the chief priests and the
> whole Council kept trying to obtain testimony
> against Jesus to put Him to death, and they were
> not finding any. For many were giving false testi-
> mony against Him, but their testimony was not con-
> sistent. (Mark 14:53, 55–56)

Some of these false witnesses twisted Jesus' words way out of context, revealing their own lack of understanding:

> "We heard Him say, 'I will destroy this temple made
> with hands, and in three days I will build another
> made without hands.'" (v. 58)

Even in this, however, the false witnesses couldn't harmonize their accusations (v. 59). So Caiaphas himself stood up and goaded Jesus, trying to get Him to say something with which they could condemn Him (v. 60). But Jesus again remained silent (v. 61a). Finally, the high priest got to the core issue:

> "Are you the Christ, the Son of the Blessed One?"
> (v. 61b)

This time Jesus did speak up, making a startling prediction:

> "I am; and you shall see the Son of Man sitting at
> the right hand of Power, and coming with the clouds
> of heaven." (v. 62)

By applying the words of Psalm 110:1 and Daniel 7:13 to Him-self, Jesus unequivocally identified Himself as equal to God. Maybe He was giving these men one final chance to recognize Him for who He was—their Messiah. All they saw, though, was that they now had what they needed to condemn Him.

> Tearing his clothes, the high priest said, "What further
> need do we have of witnesses? You have heard the
> blasphemy; how does it seem to you?" And they all
> condemned Him to be deserving of death. Some
> began to spit at Him, and to blindfold Him, and to
> beat Him with their fists, and to say to Him, "Proph-
> esy!" And the officers received Him with slaps in
> the face. (vv. 63–65)

This wasn't justice; it was vigilantism. The Jewish officials ignored the law at every turn—convening the court during the night, denying Jesus a preliminary hearing, and holding the proceedings away from their chamber. Their scheme just kept rolling on.

Trial 3: Before the Sanhedrin

In their rush to judgment, the religious rulers held a perfunctory meeting of the Sanhedrin, the supreme court of the Jews that had complete jurisdiction over all religious and theological matters. The members met in a place called the "council chamber," located in the Hall of the Hewn Stone in the temple. There they carried out their dirty business.

> When it was day, the Council of elders of the people assembled, both chief priests and scribes, and they led Him away to their council chamber, saying, "If You are the Christ, tell us." But He said to them, "If I tell you, you will not believe; and if I ask a question, you will not answer. But from now on the Son of Man will be seated at the right hand of the power of God." And they all said, "Are You the Son of God, then?" And He said to them, "Yes, I am." Then they said, "What further need do we have of testimony? For we have heard it ourselves from His own mouth." (Luke 22:66–71)

No witnesses, no proven evidence, no proper courtroom procedure —all required by law, and all completely ignored by the Sanhedrin. In probably the shortest of the six trials, lasting no more than twenty or thirty minutes, Jesus continued to be swept up in His accusers' rush to judgment.

Living Insights

John tells us that Jesus "came to His own, and those who were His own did not receive Him" (John 1:11). Understatement of the year! As we've seen, not only did the Jews "not receive Him," they openly sought to have Him killed. Can you imagine the pain Jesus felt as a result of this harsh treatment? Indeed, rejection from those we consider our "own" often hurts the most.

That's why unjust treatment from our own church members can

be so devastating. Eugene Peterson notes:

> When people become Christians, they don't at the same moment become nice. This always comes as something of a surprise. Conversion to Christ and his ways doesn't automatically furnish a person with impeccable manners and suitable morals. . . .
>
> When Christian believers gather in churches, everything that can go wrong sooner or later does. . . .
>
> So Christian churches are not, as a rule, model communities of good behavior.[5]

Describe a time when you were treated unjustly by a fellow believer.

_____

_____

_____

_____

How did you feel, and what did you do?

_____

_____

_____

Having just read how Christ behaved when His own people treated Him unjustly, how would you handle yourself differently if a similar situation came up again?

_____

_____

_____

_____

5. Eugene H. Peterson, _The Message: The New Testament in Contemporary English_ (Colorado Springs, Colo.: NavPress, 1993), pp. 337, 478.

Read 1 Peter 2:19–23. Describe all the ways in which Christ acted. What did He do? What did He *not* do?

_____

_____

_____

_____

Now jot down all the benefits you can think of for responding to injustice the way Christ did.

_____

_____

_____

_____

Peter tells us that Christ left us an example. Take a minute to pray to God, asking Him to support you as you seek to be like Christ in the face of injustice.

The Trials of Jesus Christ

Trial	Officiating Authority	Scripture	Accusation	Legality	Type	Result
1	Annas, ex-high priest of the Jews (A.D. 6–15).	John 18:13–23	Trumped-up charges of irreverence to Annas.	ILLEGAL! Held at night. No specific charges. Prejudice. Violence.	Jewish and Religious	Found guilty of irreverence and rushed to Caiaphas.
2	Caiaphas, Annas' son-in-law and high priest (A.D. 18–36).	Matthew 26:57–68 Mark 14:53–65 John 18:24	Claiming to be the Messiah, the Son of God—blasphemy (worthy of death under Jewish law).	ILLEGAL! Held at night. False witnesses. Prejudice. Violence.	Jewish and Religious	Declared guilty of blasphemy and rushed to the Sanhedrin (Jewish supreme court).
3	The Sanhedrin—seventy ruling men of Israel (their word was needed before He could be taken to Roman officials).	Mark 15:1a Luke 22:66–71	Claiming to be the Son of God—blasphemy.	ILLEGAL! Accusation switched. No witnesses. Improper voting.	Jewish and Religious	Declared guilty of blasphemy and rushed to Roman official, Pilate.
4	Pilate, governor of Judea, who was already in "hot water" with Rome (A.D. 26–36).	Matthew 27:11–14 Mark 15:1b–5 Luke 23:1–7 John 18:28–38	Treason (accusation was changed, since treason was worthy of capital punishment in Rome).	ILLEGAL! Christ was kept under arrest, although He was found innocent. No defense attorney. Violence.	Roman and Civil	Found innocent . . . but rushed to Herod Antipas; mob overruled Pilate.
5	Herod Antipas, governor of Galilee (4 B.C. – A.D. 39).	Luke 23:8–12	No accusation was made.	ILLEGAL! No grounds. Mockery in courtroom. No defense attorney. Violence.	Roman and Civil	Mistreated and mocked; returned to Pilate without decision made by Herod.
6	Pilate (second time).	Matthew 27:15–26 Mark 15:6–15 Luke 23:18–25 John 18:39–19:16	Treason, though not proven (Pilate bargained with the mob, putting Christ on a level with Barabbas, a criminal).	ILLEGAL! Without proof of guilt, Pilate allowed an innocent man to be condemned.	Roman and Civil	Found innocent, but Pilate "washed his hands" and allowed Him to be crucified.

Chapter 14

FINAL TRIALS AND
TORTURE OF JESUS

Selected Scriptures

The Jewish trials were only the beginning. As we noted in the last chapter, the Jewish leaders were unable to impose a death penalty. So, wanting Jesus gone for good, they changed their charge against Him from blasphemy to treason and turned Him over to the Roman authorities, with full knowledge that He would be crucified if found guilty.

Trial 4: Before Pilate

Jesus was first taken before Pilate, who was not known to be a fair man by any stretch of the imagination.

A Cruel Ruler

From A.D. 26 to 35, Pontius Pilate ruled as governor of Judea, an ill-fitting post for a man known to be sarcastic, unsympathetic, brutal—and decidedly anti-Semitic. But the Jews were not completely at his mercy. William Barclay gives us some insight into the tenuous relationship between this man and those he ruled.

> Philo, the great Jewish Alexandrian scholar, has a character study of Pilate—and Philo, remember, was not a Christian, but was speaking from the Jewish point of view. The Jews, Philo tells us, had threatened to exercise their right to report Pilate to the Emperor for his misdeeds. This threat "exasperated Pilate to the greatest possible degree, as he feared lest they might go on an embassy to the emperor, and might impeach him with respect to other particulars

This chapter has been adapted from "Rush to Judgment," in the study guide *Beholding Christ . . . The Lamb of God: A Study of John 15–21*, coauthored by Ken Gire, from the Bible-teaching ministry of Charles R. Swindoll (Fullerton, Calif.: Insight for Living, 1987); and "A Closer Look at Jesus' Arrest and Trials," in the study guide *A Look at the Book: Traveling the Original Route Sixty-Six*, coauthored by Lee Hough and Bryce Klabunde, from the Bible-teaching ministry of Charles R. Swindoll (Anaheim, Calif.: Insight for Living, 1994).

of his government—his corruption, his acts of insolence, his rapine, his habit of insulting people, his cruelty, his continual murders of people untried and uncondemned, and his never-ending gratuitous and most grievous inhumanity." Pilate's reputation with the Jews stank; and the fact that they could report him made his position entirely insecure.[1]

Taking advantage of this threat, the Jews turned up the heat on Pilate to convict and crucify Jesus. Unlike Jesus' Jewish trials in which the Talmudic law was ignored wholesale, the Roman trials—despite Pilate's corruption—followed the Roman code of criminal procedure to the letter. The code involved four major steps.

Accusation

All it took to begin a Roman trial was an accusation, and the Jewish officials had no qualms about providing that.

> Then they led Jesus from Caiaphas into the Praetorium, and it was early; and they themselves did not enter into the Praetorium so that they would not be defiled, but might eat the Passover. Therefore Pilate went out to them and said, "What accusation do you bring against this Man?" They answered and said to him, "If this Man were not an evildoer, we would not have delivered Him to you." (John 18:28–30)

Pilate, perhaps suspicious because they really didn't answer his question or maybe just too lazy to indulge them, tried to shoo them away:

> So Pilate said to them, "Take Him yourselves, and judge Him according to your law." (v. 31a)

But the Jews persisted, reminding him that they weren't permitted to impose the death penalty (v. 31b), a not-so-subtle hint about the outcome they desired. With the accusation leveled against Jesus, the trial progressed to the next level.

---

1. William Barclay, *The Gospel of Matthew*, vol. 2, rev. ed., The Daily Study Bible Series (Philadelphia, Pa.: Westminster Press, 1975), pp. 358–59.

Interrogation

The next step in the process was to interrogate the accused, and Pilate did just that:

> Therefore Pilate entered again into the Praetorium, and summoned Jesus and said to Him, "Are You the King of the Jews?" Jesus answered, "Are you saying this on your own initiative, or did others tell you about Me?" Pilate answered, "I am not a Jew, am I? Your own nation and the chief priests delivered You to me: what have You done?" (vv. 33–35)

This hardly seems like an interrogation—no dark room, no blinding light pointed into Jesus' eyes, no grumpy cop smoking a cigarette and drinking day-old coffee. Rather, it seems that Pilate knew less than Jesus did and simply wanted to know what was going on.

Defense

Up to this point, Jesus had been silent, or at least evasive. Given the opportunity by Pilate, Jesus now spoke the truth about Himself:

> Jesus answered, "My kingdom is not of this world. If My kingdom were of this world, then My servants would be fighting so that I would not be handed over to the Jews, but as it is, My kingdom is not of this realm." Therefore Pilate said to Him, "So You are a king?" Jesus answered, "You say correctly that I am a king. For this I have been born, and for this I have come into the world, to testify to the truth. Everyone who is of the truth hears My voice." Pilate said to Him, "What is truth?" (vv. 36–38a)

Jesus here does not offer a typical defense. He's not a criminal trying to prove His innocence, nor is He pleading for mercy. No, He's doing what He has always done—proclaiming the truth about Himself, giving people an opportunity to listen and believe . . . even a man like Pilate. A man who can't recognize the truth even when it's standing right in front of him.

Verdict

Convinced that Jesus had done no wrong and that He was no threat to the empire, Pilate tendered his verdict:

And when he [Pilate] had said this, he went out again to the Jews and said to them, "I find no guilt in Him." (v. 38)

The Jews, however, didn't give up.

But they kept on insisting, saying, "He stirs up the people, teaching all over Judea, starting from Galilee even as far as this place." (Luke 23:5)

Galilee! The name was music to Pilate's ears. It meant he could dump this mess on someone else.

When Pilate heard it [Galilee], he asked whether the man was a Galilean. And when he learned that He belonged to Herod's jurisdiction, he sent Him to Herod, who himself also was in Jerusalem at that time. (vv. 6–7)

How convenient that Jesus was a Galilean and that His ruler, Herod, just happened to be in Jerusalem! Without hesitation, Pilate handed Him over to Herod.

Trial 5: Before Herod

It was Herod Antipas, the tetrarch of Galilee, who had beheaded John the Baptist (see Matt. 14:1–12). His family was notorious throughout the region: All his brothers had been murdered by their own father, and his other relatives were also known for their iniquitous rule. Herod had heard rumors of Jesus but had never taken Him seriously, thinking Him to be nothing more than a religious sideshow. Before this Herod, Jesus now stood.

Now Herod was very glad when he saw Jesus; for he had wanted to see Him for a long time, because he had been hearing about Him and was hoping to see some sign performed by Him. And he questioned Him at some length; but He answered him nothing. And the chief priests and the scribes were standing there, accusing Him vehemently. And Herod with his soldiers, after treating Him with contempt and mocking Him, dressed Him in a gorgeous robe and sent Him back to Pilate. Now Herod and Pilate became friends with one another that very day; for before they had been enemies with each other. (Luke 23:8–12)

In the face of raucous jesting and vulgar innuendoes, Jesus stood in regal dignity, silent and composed. This infuriated His enemies, who wrapped a kingly robe around Him in mockery and returned Him to sender—but without a verdict.

Trial 6: Before Pilate Again

A sharp rap on the door brought Pilate face-to-face again with Jesus. Still trying to worm his way out of any decisive action, Pilate began to walk the tightrope between upholding justice and placating the Jewish officials.

Playing on Sympathy

> Pilate summoned the chief priests and the rulers and the people, and said to them, "You brought this man to me as one who incites the people to rebellion, and behold, having examined Him before you, I have found no guilt in this man regarding the charges which you make against Him. No, nor has Herod, for he sent Him back to us; and behold, nothing deserving death has been done by Him. Therefore, I will punish Him and release Him." (vv. 13–16)

Pilate thought he could rough up Jesus a little and then let Him go—a gross underestimation of the Jews' desire to kill Him. Beginning to realize he was dealing with determined men, Pilate tried something else.

Bargaining with Barabbas

> Now at the feast the governor was accustomed to release for the people any one prisoner whom they wanted. At that time they were holding a notorious prisoner, called Barabbas. So when the people gathered together, Pilate said to them, "Whom do you want me to release to you? Barabbas or Jesus who is called the Christ?" For he knew that because of envy they had handed Him over. (Matt. 27:15–18)

Pilate was attempting to use a convicted criminal as a bargaining chip. Matthew calls Barabbas a "notorious" prisoner. The Greek term, *episēmos*, means "bearing a mark." In other words, Barabbas was a marked man. Luke informs us that he was an insurrectionist and a murderer (Luke 23:19)—certainly deserving of the dark, dank cell he called home.

An additional pressure on Pilate came from his wife, who

> sent him a message, saying, "Have nothing to do with that righteous Man; for last night I suffered greatly in a dream because of Him." (Matt. 27:19)

In spite of the Jewish officials' manipulations and his wife's superstitions, Pilate decided to gamble that the crowd would reason rationally in weighing the obvious guilt of Barabbas against what, to Pilate, was the indiscernible crime Jesus had committed. But Pilate's roll of the dice came up snake-eyes:

> But the chief priests and the elders persuaded the crowds to ask for Barabbas and to put Jesus to death. . . . Pilate said to them, "Then what shall I do with Jesus who is called Christ?" They all said, "Crucify Him!" (vv. 20, 22)

Matthew then tells us that Pilate "took water and washed his hands in front of the crowd, saying, 'I am innocent of this Man's blood; see to that yourselves'" (v. 24). He knew he was allowing them to spill innocent blood. Yet no matter how stubbornly he washed, the crimson stain of his decision would follow him to his grave—and beyond, where he would come face-to-face with Jesus again for the last time.

In a climactic finish to the final trial, Pilate addressed the crowd.

> Now it was the day of preparation for the Passover; it was about the sixth hour. And he said to the Jews, "Behold, your King!" (John 19:14)

In a crazed crescendo, the crowd announced for all eternity its verdict:

> So they cried out, "Away with Him, away with Him, crucify Him!" Pilate said to them, "Shall I crucify your King?" The chief priests answered, "We have no king but Caesar." So he then handed Him over to them to be crucified. (vv. 15–16)

Judging Jesus Today

Do you think Pilate, Herod, and the Jews all suffered from an ancient spiritual disease that no longer hounds humanity today? Hardly. They were no different from us. Take a look around and you'll find:

- People like Pilate—concerned too much with pleasing people to do what they know is right. They know who Jesus really is, but being popular means more to them than doing the correct thing.

- People like Herod—too shallow and superficial to take spiritual realities seriously. Religion is a joke to them, something for sick people, children, and old folks.

- People like Pilate's wife—too superstitious and fearful to examine the evidence. Faith in Jesus makes them nervous, so they won't have anything to do with it.

- People like the mob—too angry and blind to listen to the truth. If Jesus was God, He wouldn't have wound up on a cross, they think.

What's your verdict about Christ? Make your choice carefully, however, for all of us will come face-to-face with Him one day. What we decide about Him now will determine how He treats us then.

Living Insights

Most of us can handle the jabs that this non-Christian world delivers to us. But how difficult it is to endure the crushing blows of injustice

- when our leaders mock our values,

- when angry interest groups attempt to assassinate our collective character,

- when our legislators stand idly by as our enemies try to muffle our voice for morality.

When unfair treatment blindsides us, our whole world starts spinning in a blur of inequities. Everything solid turns to sand. Then there are the inner ragings—anger steals our sleep, thoughts of revenge sap our joy, and doubt darkens our days. Finally, we cry out to God like the prophet Habakkuk:

How long, O Lord, will I call for help,
And You will not hear? (1:2a)

If you haven't already, let your questioning lead you to Jesus. Having felt the scourge of injustice Himself, He looks on our pain and confusion with understanding. And because of this common experience, a deeper kinship develops between Him and us. Paul called it "the fellowship of His sufferings" (Phil. 3:10). The salve for our pain is not a list of answers but an embrace of love from the One who has suffered the most.

Has injustice struck you down? Describe the situation.

_____

_____

_____

_____

In what ways do Christ and the trials He endured comfort you and give you new strength (see also Rom. 12:14–21)?

_____

_____

_____

_____

Chapter 15

DELIVERED UP TO BE CRUCIFIED

Matthew 27:27–37; John 19:16–30

A cross hung around your neck or pinned to your lapel tells the world of your faith. It also symbolizes a certain morality adhered to by Christians. And wearing it often brings a degree of respect from others.

But take that tiny piece of jewelry back in time two thousand years and try wearing it around your neck or pinning it to your toga. People would give you puzzled, suspicious looks and think you were some kind of lunatic.

Back then, the cross was a symbol, not of faith but of failure, not of morality but of lawlessness, not of respect but of unspeakable shame.

The cross was not polished and esteemed then. It loomed menacingly on the frayed hem of the city's outskirts, overlooking the garbage dumps. Made of rough-cut timbers and iron spikes, it stood ominously on the horizon . . . a sentry at attention, standing watch for any enemies of the empire . . . a stoic reminder that crimes against the state do not pay . . . a splintered vestige of barbarism in the architecture of a renowned civilization.

For Jesus—who had no room at the inn when He was born and "nowhere to lay His head" during His life (Matt. 8:20)—the cross was a final place of rest. There He raised His weary, bloodstained head and asked the Judge of the universe not for vengeance, or even for justice, but for mercy on those who crucified and cursed Him. There humanity received a second chance. And an eagerly waiting Father received His Son.

That is why, for two thousand years, the cross has captured the attention of artists, poets, philosophers, and yes, even jewelers. In the cruel brutality, they've seen something beautiful; in the rough-cut wood, something golden.

This chapter has been adapted from "The Agony of Crucifixion," in the study guide *A Look at the Book: Traveling the Original Route Sixty-Six*, coauthored by Lee Hough and Bryce Klabunde, from the Bible-teaching ministry of Charles R. Swindoll (Anaheim, Calif.: Insight for Living, 1994).

A Few Words regarding Background

Before we enter into the somber details of Jesus' crucifixion, let's first learn something of the prophetical and historical landscape surrounding it.

Biblical Predictions

Some people have the false impression that Jesus was a helpless victim of an insidious plot, a pitiful martyr whose plans were suddenly and unexpectedly terminated by a cross. Such was not the case at all. For more than nine centuries before He was lifted up to die, predictions of His death had been carefully preserved in the Scriptures.

Several passages in the Old Testament clearly prophesy the Messiah's crucifixion, one of the most prominent being Psalm 22. Here we see His pierced hands and feet (v. 16b), His bones pulled out of joint but not broken (vv. 14, 17), His clothing gambled for and divided (v. 18), the relentless, unmerciful mocking (vv. 7, 12–13), and His anguished cry to the Father (v. 1a).

Offering another poignant portrait of Christ's suffering is Isaiah, who describes the misery and torture of God's Servant (53:3, 5, 7, 11a), His being crucified with sinners (v. 12), and the Father's sovereign planning overarching it all (v. 10).

Historical Orientation

With these scenes from the ancient prophesies running through our minds, we now turn to the historical setting of the Crucifixion. The first thing to notice is the time it took place. After Pilate pronounced his verdict, he delivered Jesus over to be crucified (John 19:16; Mark 15:15), which probably occurred between 7:30 and 8:00 in the morning.

The actual sentencing took place at the judgment hall near Herod's temple. John's account helps pinpoint the location.

> Therefore when Pilate heard these words, he brought Jesus out, and sat down on the judgment seat at a place called The Pavement, but in Hebrew, Gabbatha. (John 19:13)

Recent excavations have uncovered what may be the site—a large, elevated, paved area at the northwest corner of the temple site that was part of the Castle Antonia. Roman soldiers were barracked there during Passover to maintain law and order. They probably looked down from their windows as Pilate presented Jesus to the people, seeing nothing more than great sport.

A Careful Examination of the Procedure

Step by agonizing step, we'll walk with Jesus through that momentous last day of His earthly life.

The Scourging

After Jesus' final trial before Pilate, the Roman governor had Jesus scourged (Matt. 27:26; Mark 15:15)—a cruel act that was completely unwarranted and unnecessary. Unlike Jewish scourging, in which the victim could not receive more than forty lashes (Deut. 25:1–3), Roman law was not so humane.

> A lictor, trained in the ghoulish art of torture, administered the scourging with an instrument called a flagellum. This had a round, wooden handle that had strips of leather attached to it. Into the ends of these strips were sewn pieces of bone or small iron chains. The lictor had no limit to the lashes he could deliver, and no part of the body was off-limits.[1]

Jesus was stripped and then tied to a low stone column. In vivid detail, modern-day medical doctors recreate the gruesome event.

> As the Roman soldiers repeatedly struck the victim's back with full force, the iron balls would cause deep contusions, and the leather thongs and sheep bones would cut into the skin and subcutaneous tissues. Then, as the flogging continued, the lacerations would tear into the underlying skeletal muscles and produce quivering ribbons of bleeding flesh. Pain and blood loss generally set the stage for circulatory shock. The extent of blood loss may well have determined how long the victim would survive on the cross. . . .
>
> The severe scourging, with its intense pain and appreciable blood loss, most probably left Jesus in a

---

1. See Jim Bishop, *The Day Christ Died* (New York, N.Y.: Harper and Brothers, 1957), pp. 290–91.

preshock state. Moreover, hematidrosis had rendered his skin particularly tender. The physical and mental abuse meted out by the Jews and the Romans, as well as the lack of food, water, and sleep, also contributed to his generally weakened state. Therefore, even before the actual crucifixion, Jesus' physical condition was at least serious and possibly critical.[2]

The Robe

But Jesus' suffering was far from over. The cruel soldiers, who had circled around Christ's bloody body like vultures, now moved in to pick at the remains.

> Then the soldiers of the governor took Jesus into the Praetorium and gathered the whole Roman cohort around Him. They stripped Him and put a scarlet robe on Him. (Matt. 27:27–28)

This was not a long, flowing robe. The Greek term *chlamus* indicates a short cloak worn over the shoulders. Standing there, naked from the waist down, Jesus became the object of their vulgar remarks.

The Crown

Then came more violence.

> And after twisting together a crown of thorns, they put it on His head, and a reed in His right hand; and they knelt down before Him and mocked Him, saying, "Hail, King of the Jews!" They spat on Him, and took the reed and began to beat Him on the head. After they had mocked Him, they took the scarlet robe off Him and put His own garments back on Him, and led Him away to crucify Him. (vv. 29–31)

Mocking, jeering, abusing—it's as if each soldier was trying to top the other's joke. Each took his turn spitting on Jesus . . . cursing His name . . . slapping and jabbing Him with the reed . . . punching His chest with their fists. Jesus, upon whom God would soon bestow a name that was above every other. Jesus, at

2. William D. Edwards, M.D., Wesley J. Gabel, M.Div., and Floyd E. Hosmer, M.S., A.M.I., "On the Physical Death of Jesus Christ," in *JAMA: The Journal of the American Medical Association*, March 21, 1986, pp. 1457–58.

whose name every knee would someday bow. Jesus, before whom every tongue would someday confess He is Lord (Phil. 2:9–11). But for now, humanity offered this king only spit, expletives, and fists. And Jesus bore it all with silent, patient dignity (see 1 Pet. 2:23).

The Cross

After dressing Jesus, the soldiers followed their usual course with criminals: such a victim was surrounded by four Roman soldiers and led by a centurion, all the while struggling to carry the six-foot crossbeam that would later be attached to the larger, vertical post of the cross. And so it was with Jesus. After the scourging and beating, however, He was too weak to carry the beam Himself. Matthew tells us that Simon of Cyrene was pressed into service to help Him (Matt. 27:32).

Above Jesus' head would hang a twelve-by-twenty-four-inch placard declaring His "crime": This Is Jesus the King of the Jews (v. 37). Pilate had it written not only in Hebrew, so the Jews could read it, but also in Latin for the Romans and in Greek for the more educated and sophisticated in the crowd (John 19:20). No one was going to miss the meaning of what was about to happen. It was meant as a mockery . . . yet it said more than anyone could realize (see Matt. 27:37).

The Crucifixion Itself

Crucifixion was a barbaric form of capital punishment that originated in Persia. The Persians believed that the earth was sacred to Ormuzd, the earth god, so death should not contaminate the earth. Criminals, therefore, were fastened to vertical shafts of wood by iron spikes and hung above the earth to die—from exposure, exhaustion, or suffocation. Death was painfully slow and publicly humiliating. Jim Bishop again conveys the horror.

> The executioner laid the crossbeam behind Jesus and brought him to the ground quickly by grasping his arm and pulling him backward. As soon as Jesus fell, the beam was fitted under the back of his neck and, on each side, soldiers quickly knelt on the inside of the elbows. . . . The thorns pressed against his torn scalp.
>   . . . With his right hand, the executioner probed the wrist of Jesus to find the little hollow spot. When

he found it, he took one of the square-cut iron nails . . . raised the hammer over the nail head and brought it down with force. . . .

Two soldiers grabbed each side of the crossbeam and lifted. As they pulled up, they dragged Jesus by the wrists. With every breath, he groaned. When the soldiers reached the upright, the four of them began to lift the crossbeam higher until the feet of Jesus were off the ground. The body must have writhed with pain. . . .

When the crossbeam was set firmly, the executioner . . . knelt before the cross. Two soldiers hurried to help, and each one took hold of a leg at the calf. The ritual was to nail the right foot over the left, and this was probably the most difficult part of the work. If the feet were pulled downward, and nailed close to the foot of the cross, the prisoner always died quickly. Over the years, the Romans learned to push the feet upward on the cross, so that the condemned man could lean on the nails and stretch himself upward [to breathe].[3]

The Agony and Death

Excruciating pain stabbed Christ's body as He hung on unbending nails.

The pain in his wrists was beyond bearing, and . . . muscle cramps knotted his forearms and upper arms and the pads of his shoulders; . . . his pectoral muscles at the sides of his chest were momentarily paralyzed. This induced in him an involuntary panic; for he found that while he could draw air into his lungs, he was powerless to exhale.

At once, Jesus raised himself on his bleeding feet. As the weight of his body came down on the insteps, the single nail pressed hard against the top of the wound. Slowly, steadily, Jesus was forced to raise himself higher until, for the moment, his head hid the sign which told of his crime. When his

3. Bishop, The Day Christ Died, pp. 311–12.

shoulders were on a level with his hands, breathing was rapid and easier. . . . He fought the pain in his feet in order to breathe rapidly for a few moments. Then, unable to bear the pain below, which cramped legs and thighs and wrung moans from the strongest, he let his torso sag lower and lower, and his knees projected a little at a time until, with a deep sigh, he felt himself to be hanging by the wrists. And this process must have been repeated again and again.[4]

In every crucifixion, fever would inevitably set in, inflaming the wounds and creating an insatiable thirst. Waves of hallucinations would drift the victim in and out of consciousness. In time, flies and other insects would find their way to the open wounds.

To speed up death, soldiers would break the victims' legs so they could no longer raise themselves to breathe. But with Jesus, that wouldn't be necessary. He was already dead.

So the soldiers came, and broke the legs of the first man and of the other who was crucified with Him; but coming to Jesus, when they saw that He was already dead, they did not break His legs. But one of the soldiers pierced His side with a spear, and immediately blood and water came out. (John 19:32–34)

One sign of death is the quick separation of dark red corpuscles from the thin, whitish serum of the blood, here called water. Normally, the dead do not bleed. But after death, the right auricle of the human heart fills with blood, and the membrane surrounding the heart, the pericardium, holds the watery serum. Jesus' heart must have been punctured with the spear, causing both fluids to flow from His side.

The Cross and Our Hearts

Can our hearts help but be pierced too, as we see the lover of our souls hanging in agony . . . for us? How can we respond to such devotion, such sacrifice? Perhaps, first, through the reverence of prayer. Quietly, slowly, read these words of Bernard of Clairvaux, then lift up your heart to the Lord.

---

4. Bishop, *The Day Christ Died*, p. 313.

What Thou, my Lord, hast suffered
Was all for sinners' gain;
Mine, mine was the transgression,
But Thine the deadly pain.
Lo, here I fall, my Savior;
'Tis I deserve Thy place;
Look on me with Thy favor,
Assist me with Thy grace.

What language shall I borrow
To thank Thee, dearest Friend,
For this, Thy dying sorrow,
Thy pity without end?
O make me Thine forever,
And should I fainting be,
Lord, let me never, never
Outlive my love to Thee.[5]

Living Insights

As we meditate on Christ's agonizing death and the meaning of it, each of us is faced with an inescapable question: What difference does His death make in my life, not just in some future, remote sense, but in the now and today I live in *this* moment? Author Frederick Buechner stands beside us in searching for the answer.

> He died twenty centuries ago, . . . died be-
> cause, in some way that he did not try to explain,
> his death would make all the difference, for every-
> body, until the end of time. Does it? Does it?
> It was so long ago. We do not even know what
> he looked like. (Or do we—would something in us
> recognize him if he were to appear before us?) Does
> that ancient death make any difference to people
> like us who live in a world that he could not possibly
> have imagined, a world of men, for many of whom
> God is dead? Is the death of Christ a death that

---

5. Bernard of Clairvaux, adapted by Paul Gerhardt, "O Sacred Head, Now Wounded," second and third stanzas, in *The Hymnal for Worship and Celebration* (Waco, Tex.: Word Music, 1986), no. 178.

really matters any more except in the dim way that any noble death might be said to matter?

All I can say is that I would not be writing these words unless I believed that the answer is Yes, that his death does make all the difference, even for us. I believe that by his dying he released into the world an entirely new kind of life, his kind of life, that has flowed down through the tragic centuries like water through a dry land, making alive and whole all who will only kneel to drink. And that is the only reason why it is not blasphemy to speak of the Friday of his unspeakable death as Good Friday.[6]

Take this time to examine your life and see what difference Christ's death has made and is making. What "entirely new kind of life" do you find in Him? What darkness has He overcome? What light has He brought you to? What does it mean to you to be God's reconciled child because of Christ?

_____

_____

_____

_____

_____

_____

_____

_____

_____

_____

_____

_____

6. Frederick Buechner, *The Hungering Dark* (New York, N.Y.: Seabury Press, 1969), pp. 109–10.

Chapter 16

NOT TO WORRY . . .
HE'S RISEN!

John 19:32–20:31

It was over.

The agonized straining of His body to find breath, the anguished contortions of His pain-wracked face . . . over. One final gush of water and blood, then all was still. The soldiers' spears dangled at their sides; the taunters had gone home. All was silent. Finished.

Joseph of Arimathea, a secret disciple made bold by his grief, asked Pilate for the body. Timbers creaking, lifeless flesh beyond hurting, the body was brought down and the process of burial carried out. Then the disciples, friends, and family began to drift away, each locked in a private world of anguish for the companion they had lost and for the faith they had given their lives to, yet did not now understand.

The Certainty of His Death

Later, people would say He couldn't really have been dead. He must have been unconscious or in a coma and later came to in the tomb. But the separation of the blood and water in His body (John 19:34–35) made that medically impossible. Even the soldiers knew He was really dead (vv. 32–33). More certainly than that, though, His friends knew.

> So [Joseph of Arimathea] came and took away His body. Nicodemus, who had first come to Him by night, also came, bringing a mixture of myrrh and aloes, about a hundred pounds weight. So they took the body of Jesus and bound it in linen wrappings with the spices, as is the burial custom of the Jews. (vv. 38–40)

Today, we leave the care of the dead to the undertaker, grateful for clean, quiet viewing rooms, flowers, and funereal dignity. In Jesus' time, however, family and friends were responsible for preparing the body for burial. The custom of the Jews was to wrap the entire body in strips of cloth, sprinkling a mixture of pulverized myrrh and aloe—in Jesus' case, one hundred pounds of these spices (see v. 39)—between the layers to glue them together.

Joseph and Nicodemus were friends of Jesus. Had there been the faintest pulse of life in His limp body, wouldn't they have made every effort to resuscitate Him? Of course. But they embalmed Him according to Jewish custom. One commentator added:

> Even if one could conceive them mistaken, could anyone have lain thus enveloped for the period during which He was in the grave, and life still remained? Impossible.[1]

The Finality of the Tomb

Having been prepared for burial, Jesus' body was then entombed.

> Now in the place where He was crucified there was a garden, and in the garden a new tomb in which no one had yet been laid. Therefore because of the Jewish day of preparation, since the tomb was nearby, they laid Jesus there. (vv. 41–42)

"The Jewish day of preparation" refers to the Sabbath, which began at sundown on Friday. This makeshift mortuary crew had only a short time in which to accomplish their task. To save time, Joseph of Arimathea volunteered his own tomb, a newly hewn cave of rock.

Even in death, however, Jesus' prisoner status continued. In addition to the huge stone that sealed the tomb (Matt. 27:60), Pilate gave in to pressure from the Jewish leaders and ordered a guard to keep watch outside (vv. 62–66). The chief priests and Pharisees even set a seal on the stone, which consisted of a cord stretched across the stone and fastened at each end by sealing wax or clay.[2] Anyone who broke that seal, which was official,[3] would incur the wrath of the Roman government.

---

1. Robert Jamieson, A. R. Fausset, and David Brown, *A Commentary Critical, Experimental, and Practical on the Old and New Testaments* (reprint, Grand Rapids, Mich.: William B. Eerdmans Publishing Co., 1976), vol. 3, p. 477.

2. Robert H. Mounce, *Matthew*, Good News Commentary series (San Francisco, Calif.: Harper and Row, Publishers, 1985), p. 271.

3. D. A. Carson, "Matthew," in *The Expositor's Bible Commentary*, gen. ed. Frank E. Gaebelein (Grand Rapids, Mich.: Zondervan Publishing House, Regency Reference Library, 1984), vol. 8, p. 586.

The Glory of His Resurrection

For the people who loved Jesus, who had abandoned everything to follow Him, the darkness of that first Easter morning three days later must have seemed a metaphor for their lives.

The women came first.

> Now on the first day of the week, Mary Magdalene came early to the tomb, while it was still dark. (John 20:1a)

According to Mark and Luke (Mark 16:1; Luke 24:1, 10), Mary the mother of James, Joanna, and Salome, along with a few other unnamed women, accompanied Mary Magdalene that morning. Having waited through what was surely an interminable Sabbath day, the women crept through the quiet predawn darkness toward the tomb, carrying the spices with which they hoped to anoint the body (Luke 24:1).[4]

No doubt their nerves were already on edge. They were, after all, in a cemetery, just days after witnessing the most horrific death imaginable. And an earthquake had just further jolted their world (see Matt. 28:2).[5] As if that weren't enough, the sight they came upon must have shaken them to the core.

> Looking up, they saw that the stone had been rolled away, although it was extremely large. Entering the tomb, they saw a young man sitting at the right, wearing a white robe; and they were amazed. (Mark 16:4–5)

---

4. Jesus' body had already been anointed by Joseph of Arimathea and Nicodemus (John 19:38–40). So why are the women coming to anoint Him a second time? Leon Morris tells us that "presumably this means that the burial on the Friday had had to be hurried, and when the Sabbath was over the ladies wished to complete the burial in a seemly manner." *The Gospel according to John*, rev. ed., The New International Commentary on the New Testament series (Grand Rapids, Mich.: William B. Eerdmans Publishing Co., 1995), p. 732.

5. *The Narrated Bible: In Chronological Order* harmonizes or combines the Gospel accounts to give this order of events for that resurrection morning: (1) the earthquake from the angel who rolled back the stone, (2) The women bring spices to anoint Jesus' body and wonder who will roll away the stone, (3) they find the stone has been rolled away, (4) the angel announces that Jesus is risen and tells the women to tell His disciples, (5) two more angels remind the women of Christ's prophecy about His rising, (6) Mary Magdalene tells Peter and John the amazing news. Narration by F. LaGard Smith (Eugene, Ore.: Harvest House Publishers, 1984), p. 1478.

These women had watched Nicodemus and Joseph of Arimathea roll that stone into place. They had heaved it onto its edge and maneuvered it into an inclined groove, then wedged it into place with some wood or a rock. Once Jesus' body was inside the tomb, they removed the wedge and the stone rolled into place. It was not uncommon for such a stone to weigh a ton.

Who, then, could—or would—have moved it? Not the guards; they would have feared punishment. And the disciples couldn't have because of the presence of the guards. Matthew solves the mystery.

> An angel of the Lord descended from heaven and came and rolled away the stone and sat upon it. And his appearance was like lightning, and his clothing as white as snow. (Matt. 28:2–3)

Who was this strange man in white, and what was that eerie glow? The women's questions were answered as light blinded their eyes.

> While they were perplexed about this, behold, two men[6] suddenly stood near them in dazzling clothing; and as the women were terrified and bowed their faces to the ground, the men said to them, "Why do you seek the living One among the dead? He is not here, but He has risen. Remember how He spoke to you while He was still in Galilee, saying that the Son of Man must be delivered into the hands of sinful men, and be crucified, and the third day rise again." And they remembered His words, and returned from the tomb and reported all these things to the eleven and to all the rest. (Luke 24:4–9)

It was Easter Sunday morning. And the sun had finally risen.

His First Post-Resurrection Appearances

Predictably, the disciples were skeptical.

> But these words appeared to them as nonsense, and they would not believe them. (v. 11)

---

6. Luke's noting two angels corresponds with John 20:12, while Matthew 28:2–4 and Mark 16:5 mention only one figure. There were certainly two at the tomb. Matthew's and Mark's reporting should be seen not as a mistake but as editorial license. After all, they didn't say there was *only* one angel.

Well, who would? Peter and John did exactly what we would have done: they ran to check it out.

Peter and John

> So Peter and the other disciple [John] went forth, and they were going to the tomb. The two were running together; and the other disciple ran ahead faster than Peter and came to the tomb first; and stooping and looking in, he *saw* the linen wrappings lying there, but he did not go in. (John 20:3–5, emphasis added)

Notice the word *saw*. John uses three different Greek words for it in verses 3–9, each marking a progression from physical to spiritual sight. Here in verse 5, the Greek word for *saw* is *blepei*.[7] It basically means "to note," with a strong "emphasis on the function of the eye."[8] John peered into the cave and noticed the linen wrappings, but their significance did not immediately hit him.

> And so Simon Peter also came, following him, and entered the tomb; and he *saw* the linen wrappings lying there, and the face-cloth which had been on His head, not lying with the linen wrappings, but rolled up in a place by itself. (vv. 6–7, emphasis added)

Next came Simon Peter, puffing up behind John. Shouldering past John into the tomb, he "saw" what John had seen but in a different way. The Greek word this time is *theōrei*,[9] from which we get our word *theorize*. Peter saw something he wasn't expecting, and it stopped him in his tracks. Eyes narrowed, brow furrowed, he studied it and pondered what it could mean. Merrill Tenney offers some insight into what it was that so arrested Peter's attention.

> Why should the condition of the graveclothes excite Peter's amazement? . . .

7. Edwin A. Blum, "John," in *The Bible Knowledge Commentary*, New Testament edition, ed. John F. Walvoord and Roy B. Zuck (Colorado Springs, Colo.: Chariot Victor Publishing, 1983), p. 342.

8. Gerhard Kittel and Gerhard Friedrich, eds., *Theological Dictionary of the New Testament*, translated and abridged in one volume by Geoffrey W. Bromiley (1985; reprint, Grand Rapids, Mich.: William B. Eerdmans Publishing Co., 1992), p. 706.

9. Blum, "John," p. 342.

There is a strong hint that the clothes were not folded as if Jesus had unwound them and then deposited them in two neat piles on the shelf. The word used to describe the napkin or head cloth does not connote a flat folded square like a table napkin, but a ball of cloth bearing the appearance of being rolled around an object that was no longer there. The wrappings were in position where the body had lain, and the head cloth was where the head had been, separated from the others by the distance from armpits to neck. The shape of the body was still apparent in them, but the flesh and bone had disappeared.[10]

Empty graveclothes—but their shape intact, like the shell of a locust still clinging to a tree, or an opened cocoon still dangling from a leaf. Tenney adds, "The tomb had not been opened to let Jesus out, but to let in the disciples. Transformed by the resurrection, He had passed through the grave clothes, leaving like an outworn chrysalis the cerements of the tomb for the vestments of glory."[11] Peter could not figure it out, but John was beginning to.

So the other disciple who had come first to the tomb then also entered, and he *saw* and believed. For as yet they did not understand the Scripture, that He must rise again from the dead. So the disciples went away again to their own homes. (vv. 8–10, emphasis added)

This time the word *saw, eiden* in Greek,[12] means "to perceive," "to realize."[13] In other words, it all fell into place, it clicked. John stood next to Peter gazing at that odd sight, and the light came on. "Peter, Peter, He's been raised from the dead! He's alive!" John may not have understood Jesus' Resurrection as foretold by Scripture (v. 9), but what he saw, he believed.

Mary Magdalene

Mary, too, returned to the tomb. She retraced her steps alone,

10. Merrill C. Tenney, *The Reality of the Resurrection* (New York, N.Y.: Harper and Row, Publishers, 1963), pp. 118–19.

11. Merrill C. Tenney, *John: The Gospel of Belief* (1976; reprint, Grand Rapids, Mich.: William B. Eerdmans Publishing Co., 1989), p. 281.

12. Blum, "John," p. 342.

13. Kittel and Friedrich, eds., *Theological Dictionary of the New Testament*, p. 710.

drawn irresistibly to the place she had last seen her Lord. Troubled and confused, she stood at the mouth of the empty tomb.

> But Mary was standing outside the tomb weep-
> ing; and so, as she wept, she stooped and looked into
> the tomb; and she saw two angels in white sitting,
> one at the head and one at the feet, where the body
> of Jesus had been lying. And they said to her,
> "Woman, why are you weeping?" She said to them,
> "Because they have taken away my Lord, and I do
> not know where they have laid Him." (vv. 11–13)

Maybe the morning was hazy with fog, or maybe her vision was blurred by tears, or maybe Jesus was just the last person she expected to see. But when she turned around, she didn't recognize the One for whom her heart ached.

> When she had said this, she turned around and saw
> Jesus standing there, and did not know that it was
> Jesus. Jesus said to her, "Woman, why are you weep-
> ing? Whom are you seeking?" Supposing Him to be
> the gardener, she said to Him, "Sir, if you have car-
> ried Him away, tell me where you have laid Him,
> and I will take Him away." Jesus said to her, "Mary!"
> She turned and said to Him in Hebrew, "Rabboni!"
> (which means, Teacher). Jesus said to her, "Stop
> clinging to Me, for I have not yet ascended to the
> Father; but go to My brethren and say to them, 'I
> ascend to My Father and your Father, and My God
> and your God.'" Mary Magdalene came, announcing
> to the disciples, "I have seen the Lord," and that He
> had said these things to her. (vv. 14–18)

The Disciples

It wouldn't be long before the rest of Jesus' friends saw Him too. That evening, the disciples were huddled in a locked room, fearful of the Jews, when suddenly Jesus appeared in their midst. Dumbstruck, they stared as He showed them His hands and His side . . . and then erupted in cries of joy! But one disciple was not present for this astounding event. When he did join them, doubt was evident in his eyes.

> But Thomas, one of the twelve, called Didymus, was not with them when Jesus came. So the other disciples were saying to him, "We have seen the Lord!" But he said to them, "Unless I see in His hands the imprint of the nails, and put my finger into the place of the nails, and put my hand into His side, I will not believe." (vv. 24–25)

For eight days after this event (see v. 26), the other disciples were joyously linked in the experience they had shared. Thomas must have felt like such an outsider. He wanted to believe, but he hadn't been there. Where he *had* been was on the hill that Friday. What he *had* seen was the body, hanging limp on the cross. The skepticism and logic that may have been his natural approach to life kept him shaking his head: "Wishful thinking. It's what we'd all like to be true."

Graciously, Jesus gave Thomas the proof he needed. And notice, His words were gentle, direct, and, above all, convincing.

> After eight days His disciples were again inside, and Thomas with them. Jesus came, the doors having been shut, and stood in their midst and said, "Peace be with you." Then He said to Thomas, "Reach here with your finger, and see My hands; and reach here your hand and put it into my side; and do not be unbelieving, but believing. Thomas answered and said to him, "My Lord and my God!" (vv. 26–28)

With these words, Thomas uttered the climactic words of John's gospel. For John's purpose in writing his Gospel was

> so that you may believe that Jesus is the Christ, the Son of God; and that believing you may have life in His name. (v. 31)

Living Insights

Frank Morison was something of a Thomas. A well-educated British lawyer, his thinking had been shaped by the German critics, Oxford professor Matthew Arnold, and biologist Dr. Thomas Huxley—all of whom openly denied even the possibility of miracles.

Morison, in an effort to disprove the Christian belief that Jesus was miraculously raised from the dead, set out to write a book. Little did he suspect that the book he ended up writing would be so radically different from the book he had planned. *Who Moved the Stone?* turned out to be a defense of the bodily resurrection of Christ. In his own words, he "discovered one day that not only could he no longer write the book as he had once conceived it, but that he would not if he could."[14] And this change of heart happened, "not suddenly, as in a flash of insight or inspiration, but slowly, almost imperceptibly, by the very stubbornness of the facts themselves."[15]

Is there a Thomas or a Morison in your life? Maybe someone you've been trying to convince about the validity of Christianity, only to be met with heels-in-the-sand skepticism?

If so, what has been your approach to them? Based on Jesus' approach to Thomas, what do you think Jesus would have you do differently?

Perhaps you see a little bit of Thomas in yourself. How do you think Jesus feels about this? What do you think He might like to say to you?

---

14. Frank Morison, *Who Moved the Stone?* (Downers Grove, Ill.: InterVarsity Press, 1971), preface.

15. Morison, *Who Moved the Stone?*, preface.

Chapter 17

ENCOUNTERING JESUS ALONG LIFE'S ROAD
Luke 24:13–35

O ne Week. It's a rather inconsequential unit of time. Fifty-two of them are packed into a year, thousands into a lifetime. We dispense them without much thought: "I won't be gone too long on vacation, just a week." "Summer's going fast. In a couple of weeks, school starts." "You won't have to wear the bandage long— a few weeks at most."

Yet think of the earthshaking events that took place in the space of one week at the end of Jesus' life:

- After His triumphal entry into Jerusalem on Sunday (Luke 19:28–44), He drove the profit-mongers from the temple. Then He spent His next few days instructing His followers about the kingdom of God and debating the religious leaders (chaps. 20–21).

- Following this was a period of preparation: Judas prepared to betray the Lord, the disciples made the arrangements for the Passover, and Jesus readied His men for the coming conflict (22:1–38).

- A time of supplication came next, with Jesus praying feverishly in Gethsemane (vv. 39–46).

- Judas' kiss set in motion the events of the Crucifixion, in which Jesus endured six unjust trials and the agony of death on the cross (22:47–23:56).

- Then on Sunday morning came the Resurrection—Jesus' glorious triumph over sin and death.

Surely, this was a week like no other—one that remains fixed at the pinnacle of history. And it's not over yet.

This chapter has been adapted from two study guides from the Bible-teaching ministry of Charles R. Swindoll: *The Consummation of Something Miraculous: A Study of Luke 16:19–24:53*, coauthored by Bryce Klabunde (Anaheim, Calif.: Insight for Living, 1995), pp. 126–29, 133–34; and *Christ at the Crossroads*, coauthored by Lee Hough (Anaheim, Calif.: Insight for Living, 1991), pp. 150–55.

In our last lesson, we ran with the women from the empty tomb to tell the disciples the wonderful news. From there, we sped forward in time to watch the reactions of the disciples when they saw for themselves that Jesus was indeed alive. But between those two momentous events were some other occurrences that are well worth eavesdropping on. Today we'll take a look at the first one.

The Emmaus Experience

It had been an agonizing week for Jesus and an excruciating one for His followers. Devastated and confused, they thought it was the end when that stone was rolled into place, sealing off with finality the Man who was to have changed their world. Then, three days later, the women brought the news that the grave was empty and Jesus was alive! Everyone else had yet to see Him, though. What was going on? Bewildered, wrung out from wild swings of emotion, unsure of what to believe, two of them headed away from Jerusalem to the quieter village of Emmaus. But the road there was hardly the end; for these two, it was just the beginning.

I Once Was Blind . . .

> And behold, two of them were going that very day to a village named Emmaus, which was about seven miles from Jerusalem. And they were talking with each other about all these things which had taken place. While they were talking and discussing, Jesus Himself approached and began traveling with them. But their eyes were prevented from recognizing Him. (Luke 24:13–16)

One nice thing about a resurrected body is the lack of physical restrictions. Jesus was able to just appear beside these men. But, preoccupied as they were with their thoughts and conversation, they didn't notice His unusual manner of approach; they just assumed He was another walker catching up to them.

> And He said to them, "What are these words that you are exchanging with one another as you are walking?" And they stood still, looking sad. (v. 17)

Oblivious to the truly surprising thing happening then and there, the two men are shocked that anyone could have missed the events of this turbulent week.

137

One of them, named Cleopas, answered and said to Him, "Are You the only one visiting Jerusalem and unaware of the things which have happened here in these days?" And He said to them, "What things?" (vv. 18–19a)

Notice, Jesus didn't just barge in with all the answers. Instead, He asks a question and listens to His disciples. And His question drew an answer from the two.

And they said to Him, "The things about Jesus the Nazarene, who was a prophet mighty in deed and word in the sight of God and all the people, and how the chief priests and our rulers delivered Him to the sentence of death, and crucified Him. But we were hoping that it was He who was going to redeem Israel. Indeed, besides all this, it is the third day since these things happened. But also some women among us amazed us. When they were at the tomb early in the morning, and did not find His body, they came, saying that they had also seen a vision of angels who said that He was alive. Some of those who were with us went to the tomb and found it just exactly as the women also had said; but Him they did not see." (vv. 19b–24)

But Now I See!

The mixture of disappointment, doubt, and confusion they feel is evident in their words. Surely it's all Jesus can do not to burst out, "Come on, guys, we've been over this a hundred times." But He holds His tongue and answers them only as a knowledgeable stranger might.

And He said to them, "O foolish men and slow of heart to believe in all that the prophets have spoken! Was it not necessary for the Christ to suffer these things and to enter into His glory?" Then beginning with Moses and with all the prophets, He *explained* to them the things concerning Himself in all the Scriptures. (vv. 25–27, emphasis added)

What a great moment—Christ opening the Scriptures about Himself! The word "explained," *diermēneuō*, comes from the Greek root from which we get our term *hermeneutics*—the principles or study of biblical interpretation. It indicates that Jesus went back to the books of Moses, Genesis through Deuteronomy, through all of the prophets, ending with Malachi, and interpreted them for these two disciples. He showed them the truth about Himself—the main theme—in all of Scripture. And they began to understand.

As Jesus speaks, a spark of truth flashes through their dark despair. Soon a flame of hope ignites. By the time they reach Emmaus, their hearts are ablaze. Eager to hear more, they urge this amazing Teacher not to leave. "Stay with us," they press Him (v. 29). And so together, they sit down for a meal, and Jesus takes the bread, blesses it, breaks it, and gives it to them (v. 30).

Maybe these men had been in the crowd when Jesus fed the five thousand, and that image of broken bread somehow jogged their memories. Or maybe they finally noticed the nail scars on His wrists. Maybe Jesus just chose then to open their eyes. Whatever it was, at that moment, they knew. It was Jesus who was with them. They must have turned to each other, first in amazement, then . . . mystified.

> Then their eyes were opened and they recognized Him; and He vanished from their sight. (v. 31)

Imagine their astonishment as, at once, their eyes widen and they blurt out, "You're Je—" . . . and, blink—He disappears!

> They said to one another, "Were not our hearts burning within us while He was speaking to us on the road, while he was *explaining* the Scriptures to us?" (v. 32, emphasis added)

This "explaining" has a different meaning from the one in verse 27. Here it means "open," just as their eyes were "opened" in verse 31. It indicates that Scripture remains incomprehensible until we see the illuminating truth of Jesus. It's like trying to put together a puzzle without the picture on the box. Without seeing Christ in the Bible, we travel blindly through a maze of meaningless ideas, people, and events. For He is the key that unlocks the truth and opens eternal mysteries for us.

The two men cannot wait until morning to share their experience with the disciples.

> And they got up that very hour and returned to

Jerusalem, and found gathered together the eleven and those who were with them, saying, "The Lord has really risen and has appeared to Simon." They began to relate their experiences on the road and how He was recognized by them in the breaking of the bread. (vv. 33–35)

God's Majestic Son throughout Scripture

What exactly did Jesus teach the two as they walked along the Emmaus road? He revealed to them that each book of the Scriptures contained truth about Him. Such knowledge can encourage us too.

Books of the Bible	Names of Christ
Genesis	Seed of the Woman
Exodus	Passover Lamb
Leviticus	Atoning Sacrifice
Numbers	Bronze Serpent
Deuteronomy	Promised Prophet
Joshua	Unseen Captain
Judges	Our Deliverer
Ruth	Kinsman Redeemer
1 and 2 Samuel, 1 and 2 Kings, 1 and 2 Chronicles	Promised King
Ezra and Nehemiah	Restorer of the Nation
Esther	Our Advocate
Job	Our Redeemer
Psalms	Our All in All
Proverbs	Our Pattern
Ecclesiastes	Our Goal
Song of Solomon	Our Beloved
All the Prophets	Coming Prince of Peace
Matthew	Christ, the King
Mark	Christ, the Servant
Luke	Christ, the Son of Man
John	Christ, the Son of God

Books of the Bible	Names of Christ
Acts	Christ Ascended, Seated, Sending
All the Letters	Christ Indwelling, Filling
Revelation	Christ Returning, Reigning

But there's more—in the thirty-nine Old Testament books, Christ is in the shadows, seen in analogies and pictures, in types and rituals. He is prophesied and anticipated. The twenty-seven New Testament books complete the Old, revealing Christ in person, in truth and reality, in the present and acknowledged.

Our Own Emmaus Experiences

Everyone faces times of confusion and doubt. They're part of life. The good news is that, just as He did all those centuries ago, Jesus walks our Emmaus roads with us. He matches His stride to ours and reminds us of the reasons to keep going. In fact, His words to those ancient travelers hold messages for us as well.

First, *remember what you already know.* The two travelers were discouraged because they'd forgotten all they had been taught— they had let their present circumstances drive the truth from their minds. As Jesus took them back over the familiar ground of the Scriptures, their hopelessness lifted. When we're discouraged, there's nothing like immersing ourselves in the Word to remind us of the hope available to us.

Second, *expect the unexpected.* The two travelers expected Jesus to become an earthly king and to restore Israel to national prominence. They didn't realize that He was building an even greater spiritual kingdom. God sometimes solves our problems in unexpected ways. To keep from getting frustrated, we need to remember that He doesn't always work the way we would—and then we need to trust Him.

Living Insights

William Barclay draws upon the story we've been studying to highlight one of the Lord's most precious qualities.

> [This story] tells us of the ability of Jesus to make sense of things. The whole situation seemed to these

two men to have no explanation. Their hopes and dreams were shattered. There is all the poignant, wistful, bewildered regret in the world in their sorrowing words, "We were hoping that he was the one who was going to rescue Israel." They were the words of men whose hopes were dead and buried. Then Jesus came and talked with them, and the meaning of life became clear and the darkness became light. A story-teller makes one of his characters say to the one with whom he has fallen in love, "I never knew what life meant until I saw it in your eyes." It is only in Jesus that, even in the bewildering times, we learn what life means.[1]

Have you been wandering down an Emmaus road, trying to piece together a shattered dream? Groping for answers but only finding more questions? If so, describe the darkness that is troubling you.

_____

_____

_____

_____

_____

_____

   Wouldn't it be wonderful for Christ Himself to page through the Scriptures with you to show you the way back to hope? We may not have His physical presence, but we do have the Holy Spirit. Perhaps, in your search for answers, you've forgotten to look to the source of all knowledge. Take a few moments to ask for the Spirit's wisdom as you look to the Bible for help. Perhaps He'll guide you to a psalm or a proverb or a verse in one of the epistles. Wherever He takes you, remember Paul's prayer for all believers:

   [I pray] that the God of our Lord Jesus Christ, the

1. William Barclay, *The Gospel of Luke*, rev. ed., The Daily Study Bible Series (Philadelphia, Pa.: Westminster Press, 1975), p. 295.

Father of glory, may give to you a spirit of wisdom and of revelation in the knowledge of Him. I pray that the eyes of your heart may be enlightened, so that you will know what is the hope of His calling, what are the riches of the glory of His inheritance in the saints, and what is the surpassing greatness of His power toward us who believe. (Eph. 1:17–19a)

To what Scripture is the Spirit leading you, and what does it teach you?

_____

_____

_____

_____

_____

_____

_____

_____

_____

Chapter 18

LISTENING TO
JESUS BESIDE THE SEA
John 21:1–22

Gone Fishing.

How many times have you wanted to hang that sign on your door? Maybe when there's a lull in business. Maybe when job pressures hem you in and you feel trapped. Or maybe when a wave of nostalgia washes over you one warm summer day and you yearn to go barefoot at the old fishing hole where so many fond memories are pooled.

Maybe those were some of the disciples' thoughts after Jesus died. Perhaps that's why they took the day off and went fishing. The ministry, for all practical purposes, had shut down. Sure, the Resurrection brought a flurry of renewed optimism, but it also raised a number of questions to which they had no answers—like, "Now what?"

Perhaps the disciples felt hemmed in by the corruption of the Pharisees and chief priests, not to mention the impending threat of the Roman government. After all, Jesus had warned them that if the world persecuted Him, it would certainly persecute them too.

Perhaps, as they sat by the Sea of Galilee and listened to the rhythm of the waves, they felt their spirits ebbing nostalgically back to the past. When Peter said, "I'm going fishing," thoughts of his past came back to him—thoughts of when Jesus first recruited him.

> As He was going along by the Sea of Galilee, He saw Simon and Andrew, the brother of Simon, casting a net in the sea; for they were fishermen. And Jesus said to them, "Follow Me, and I will make you become fishers of men." Immediately they left their nets and followed Him. (Mark 1:16–18)

For the next three years, Peter and the other fishermen learned from Jesus, watching as He calmed storms, walked on water, and

This chapter has been adapted from the study guide *Beholding Christ . . . The Lamb of God: A Study of John 15–21*, coauthored by Ken Gire, from the Bible-teaching ministry of Charles R. Swindoll (Fullerton, Calif.: Insight for Living, 1987), pp. 100–10.

cast His saving net into humanity's sea. But now, in the wake of His death and Resurrection, all was calm, and the disciples returned to their old vocation—back to Galilee and their nets. It is there we find them in John 21.

One Last Catch

The disciples were back where it all started. What a perfect spot for Jesus to appear.

> After these things Jesus manifested Himself again to the disciples at the Sea of Tiberias, and He manifested Himself in this way. Simon Peter, and Thomas called Didymus, and Nathanael of Cana in Galilee, and the sons of Zebedee, and two others of His disciples were together. (John 21:1–2)

The scene opens on the shores of Galilee's sea, also known as the Sea of Tiberias. The disciples find themselves enveloped in quiet, melancholy darkness. Few words are spoken. No one knows what to say. One of them skips a rock. Another mindlessly picks up a handful of sand and sifts it through his fingers. Finally, Peter speaks up.

> Simon Peter said to them, "I am going fishing." They said to him, "We will also come with you." They went out and got into the boat; and that night they caught nothing. (v. 3)

How frustrated the disciples must have felt when, time after time, their nets came up empty. They were fishermen by trade, and they couldn't even catch a minnow! At the height of their frustration and exhaustion, Jesus quietly appears to them.

> But when the day was now breaking, Jesus stood on the beach; yet the disciples did not know that it was Jesus. So Jesus said to them, "Children, you do not have any fish, do you?" They answered Him, "No." And he said to them, "Cast the net on the right-hand side of the boat and you will find a catch." So they cast, and then they were not able to haul it in because of the great number of fish. (20:4–6)

Imagine their surprise when they pull up the net brimming with

145

fish, each one a keeper (v. 11). Imagine their even greater surprise when they recognized who was standing on the bank.

> Therefore that disciple whom Jesus loved said to Peter, "It is the Lord." So when Simon Peter heard that it was the Lord, he put his outer garment on (for he was stripped for work), and threw himself into the sea. (v. 7)

That's Peter for you—never one to hold back, and he's more glad to see his Savior than he's ever been to see anyone on earth. So he heads for shore the fastest way he can think of, fish forgotten. Straining at the oars and net, the others follow.

> But the other disciples came in the little boat, for they were not far from the land, but about one hundred yards away, dragging the net full of fish. (v. 8)

One Last Breakfast

As Peter and the others reach the shore, they find a meal prepared and a table set. This was no chance meeting, but one carefully planned by the Lord.

> So when they got out on the land, they saw a charcoal fire already laid and fish placed on it, and bread. Jesus said to them, "Bring some of the fish which you have now caught." Simon Peter went up and drew the net to land, full of large fish, a hundred and fifty-three; and although there were so many, the net was not torn. Jesus said to them, "Come and have breakfast." None of the disciples ventured to question Him, "Who are You?" knowing that it was the Lord. Jesus came and took the bread and gave it to them, and the fish likewise. (vv. 9–13)

It must have felt like old times, sitting with Jesus, eating and talking together. Their voices murmur across the stretch of deserted beach. Smoke curls above the fire. The radiant heat of the crackling wood begins to chase away the morning chill. It's an intimate moment. Every word that falls from Jesus' lips feeds their hungry hearts. His presence reminds them of that which they had momentarily ignored—their lives as "fishers of *men*."

One Last Message

As the sun dawns on that placid sea and the disciples warm themselves by the fire, Jesus probes a recent wound in Peter's heart.

Restoration

> So when they had finished breakfast, Jesus said to Simon Peter, "Simon, son of John, do you love Me more than these?" He said to Him, "Yes, Lord; You know that I love You." He said to him, "Tend My lambs." He said to him a second time, "Simon, son of John, do you love Me?" He said to Him, "Yes, Lord; You know that I love You." He said to him, "Shepherd My sheep." He said to him the third time, "Simon, son of John, do you love Me?" Peter was grieved because He said to Him the third time, "Do you love Me?" And he said to Him, "Lord, You know all things; You know that I love You." Jesus said to him, "Tend My sheep." (vv. 15–17)

Three times Jesus asks the same question—one for each of Peter's denials. And He asks it, not of Peter the Rock, but of Simon, the name some speculate means "shifting one." With the use of this name, Jesus takes Peter back to the beginning of their relationship —not to demote but to rebuild the foundation. Let's watch how He does it.

Notice two things in the first question, "Do you love Me more than these?" First, there is no clear reference for the word *these*. It could refer to "these men," meaning the disciples, or it could mean "these fish," referring to Peter's vocation. Possibly it refers to both.

The second thing to notice is the word *love*. Jesus actually spoke Aramaic, but John was directed to write his Gospel account in Greek, a much more precise language. The Greek term used here is *agapao*, the highest, most all-encompassing form of love. But the word Peter uses in response is *phileo*, the term for friendship: "You know I'm fond of You, Lord; we're friends." Peter remembers his earlier, adamant devotion (13:37)—and his subsequent betrayal. Perhaps kicking at the sand with his toe, face averted, he tries to be more honest this time. But even in the face of admitted inadequacy, Christ still has a role for Peter to fulfill—"Tend My lambs."

The interview isn't over, however. Jesus repeats His question, this time dropping "more than these" but keeping *agapao*. Deleting the last phrase narrows the issue; it's just about Peter and where the Lord really fits in his life. Again Peter responds with less than what Christ asks for ("I *phileo* you"), but Jesus reiterates His commission: "Shepherd My sheep."

In the final question, Jesus uses the same term for love that Peter used—*phileo:* "Simon, are you just fond of Me?" Grieved, yet truthful, Peter responds, "You already know everything. You know that I am fond of You, yet You also know that my love is flawed." Remarkably, Christ's commission remains consistent: "You're right; I do know. But I still want you to tend My sheep. I haven't given up on you; I haven't put you on the shelf."

Prediction

What relief Peter must have felt! But the news isn't all reassuring. His future holds a purpose and a mission, but that mission will end in a grim finish.

> "Truly, truly, I say to you, when you were younger, you used to gird yourself and walk wherever you wished; but when you grow old, you will stretch out your hands and someone else will gird you, and bring you where you do not wish to go." Now this He said signifying by what kind of death he would glorify God. (vv. 18–19a)

The picture Jesus paints in the first part of verse 18 is that of a self-assured youth, strong-willed, capable, determined, and independent. But in the latter part of that verse, the picture changes radically. At the end, Peter is not in charge of his own destiny or even his own daily routines.

In the third volume of Eusebius's *Ecclesiastical History*, the first-century historian notes that Peter was martyred around A.D. 61. First, he saw his wife crucified before his own eyes, and then, with a willing heart, he submitted himself to the cross. But feeling unworthy to die in the same manner as his Lord, he asked that he be crucified upside down.

One Last Lesson

True to his nature, Peter prompts Jesus to teach him one last lesson.

> And when He had spoken this, He said to him, "Follow Me!" Peter, turning around, saw the disciple

whom Jesus loved following them; the one who also had leaned back on His bosom at the supper and said, "Lord, who is the one who betrays You?" So Peter seeing him said to Jesus, "Lord, and what about this man?" (vv. 19b–21)

Jesus and Peter have spent the last several minutes in a narrow focus on their own relationship. But now, glancing over his shoulder, Peter sees John. Like siblings everywhere, he can't resist asking, "What about John?" Like a charcoaled ember inflamed by a fanning breeze, Peter's old weakness for comparison flares up. And Jesus responds like any parent, "Mind your own business!" (v. 22).

Looking Back on the Lessons

What can we take away from Jesus' time with the disciples? What principles can we draw?

First, *when the Lord offers an opportunity to transform futility into fruitfulness, be open to change.* The disciples had been casting their nets all night without a single catch. Then Jesus told them to cast on the other side of the boat, and they harvested a bounty of fish. When we're in the middle of a futile effort and God gives us an opportunity for change, we need to be open to His leading.

Second, *when He moves you in a new and challenging direction, expect to do some soul-searching.* Peter was on the verge of a new challenge—to lead the church without Jesus' physical presence to help him. But first, Jesus led him through some soul-searching. Like Peter, we need to be realistic about our abilities and level of commitment—yet also be willing to go forward, trusting in God's provision.

Third, *as you follow Christ, don't compare yourself with others.* Jesus' plan for you is individual, tailored just for you. Don't waste time and energy worrying about what He has planned for others. It will only distract you from what God has asked you to do.

Living Insights

Have you ever stopped to think about the people God uses to accomplish His purpose? The A-team, right? The heavy hitters— people like Elijah, Noah, Peter, David, Jonah, Abraham, and Moses. Yet all of those people failed, and some, tragically.

When we fail, Satan is quick to run us into the ground and

trample any remaining vestige of self-worth. In fact, that's what the word *devil* means—"the accuser." He'll have us call ourselves every name in the book: *fool, idiot, loser, failure*.

Like the disciples at the sea, are you standing on a similar shore, casting nets in some quiet cove, away from the mainstream of life where God wants you? What failure or shortcoming has led you to this place?

_____

_____

_____

What's keeping you from jumping back into the mainstream?

_____

_____

_____

True love "does not take into account a wrong suffered" (1 Cor. 13:5b). Jesus doesn't sit in heaven sharpening His red pencil, ready to jot down every mistake we make. Peter himself tells us, years later, that "love covers a multitude of sins" (1 Pet. 4:8). And where do you think he learned that lesson? Right on the beach where Jesus picked him up and dusted him off.

When you've fallen flat on your face, when you're down with the sand in your eyes and mouth, remember that Satan is the one who's going to kick you—or cause you to kick yourself. Jesus will be the one reaching out His hand to restore you. All you have to do is take His hand, as Peter did, and walk with Him.

Chapter 19

CHALLENGED BY JESUS ON THE MOUNTAIN

Matthew 28:16–20; Mark 16:14–16; Acts 1:6–8

Last words—those final, precious thoughts verbalized just prior to death. Some of them can be humorous, as was the case with Ethan Allen (1738–89), a U.S. patriot and leader of the Green Mountain Boys during the Revolutionary War:

> Allen lay ill. The doctor examined him and said, "General, I fear the angels are waiting for you."
> "Waiting, are they?" said the bluff frontiersman.
> "Waiting, are they? Well—let 'em wait."[1]

Other final words can be tragic. Julius Caesar, one of the most controversial characters in history, spoke what may be the most famous last words of all time. After a spectacular life in which he purged the Roman Empire of corruption, created the Julian calendar we use today, brought Britain under Roman rule, and consolidated power under the Caesar name, Julius was stabbed to death by his own friends. When he saw his beloved friend Brutus among the conspirators, he said, *"Et tu, Brute?"*[2] ("You too, Brutus?").

Final words can also relay thoughts of great importance, communicating a person's highest priority. Such was the case with our Lord and Savior Jesus Christ. After He died, rose from the grave, and appeared to many different people, Jesus visited His disciples and spoke to them one last time before ascending to Paradise:

> "Go therefore and make disciples of all the nations, baptizing them in the name of the Father and the

---

This chapter has been adapted from "My Commitment to Christ's Commission," in the study guide *What It Takes to Win*, coauthored by Bryce Klabunde, from the Bible-teaching ministry of Charles R. Swindoll (Anaheim, Calif.: Insight for Living, 1993).

1. Ethan Allen, as quoted in *The Little, Brown Book of Anecdotes*, gen. ed. Clifton Fadiman (Boston, Mass.: Little, Brown and Co., 1985), p. 15.

2. Julius Caesar, *The Little, Brown Book of Anecdotes*, p. 95; and *The Concise Columbia Electronic Encyclopedia* (Columbia University Press, 1994). On-line. Available at http://www.historychannel.com. Accessed: November 30, 1999.

Son and the Holy Spirit, teaching them to observe all that I commanded you; and lo, I am with you always, even to the end of the age." (Matt. 28:19–20)

These final words from God's majestic Son are commonly called the Great Commission—and they're not limited to just His eleven disciples. He directs them to all His disciples, of every nation and every age. From His words we can make four observations that will help us as we seek to obey His charge.

Four Observations regarding the Great Commission

Three men recorded Jesus' Great Commission in Scripture: Matthew, Mark, and Luke. Let's compare and analyze their accounts to make our observations.

1. Jesus Talked to Ordinary People Who Knew Him

The eleven disciples proceeded to Galilee, to the mountain which Jesus had designated. When they saw Him, they worshiped Him; but some were doubtful. And Jesus came up and spoke to them. (Matt. 28:16–18a)

Afterward He appeared to the eleven themselves as they were reclining at the table. (Mark 16:14a)

So when they had come together . . . (Acts 1:6a)

When Jesus gave His commission, He spoke to ordinary people who knew Him well. His manner was casual and natural; His disciples weren't aware that He had given them what we so loftily term the Great Commission. He simply talked to them. And those who heard His words certainly weren't heroes of the faith. "Some were doubtful," Matthew wrote (28:17). Mark said Jesus needed to reproach some for their "unbelief and hardness of heart" (16:14b). According to Luke, they had a list of questions right up to the very end (Acts 1:6b). But into the unsure hands of these doubting men, Jesus passed the baton of truth.

What would they do with this baton? Jesus didn't give them any do-it-yourself miracle kits to transform them into super-missionaries. He alone—not His followers—had been given all authority "in heaven and on earth" (Matt. 28:18). The disciples didn't have glowing halos, and they didn't suddenly become serene saints reposing piously. They were just regular folks who knew and loved Jesus—and that's all they needed to be.

2. Jesus Stated the Plan Clearly and Simply

Jesus' objective was clear and simple too: "Make disciples" (Matt. 28:19a). *Make disciples, mathēteuō* in Greek, is the main verb in His statement. It is obviously related to the noun "disciples," *mathētēs*, which has a rich meaning.

> *Mathētēs* is used for those who direct their minds to something. It then denotes the "pupil" . . . as one engaged in learning.
> . . . A basic feature of NT discipleship is that . . . Jesus takes the initiative. . . . This differs sharply from rabbinic practice, in which it is the student's duty to find a teacher. . . .
> . . . A unique aspect of NT discipleship is that it is commitment to the person of Jesus. His teaching has force only when there is first this commitment to his person. . . . As distinct from the customary rabbi, or indeed the Greek teacher, Jesus offers himself rather than his outstanding gifts, and claims allegiance to himself rather than to a cause that he represents. . . . For [the disciples] the decisive thing is not just to appropriate intellectually but to obey.[3]

All of Jesus' other action words—*go, baptizing,* and *teaching* — support His commission to (1) actively call people (2) to a living commitment to Himself (3) in which they continually learn about and grow in Him (see also 2 Pet. 3:18).

3. Jesus Was Intense about Involvement but Relaxed regarding Method

Jesus didn't hand His disciples an evangelism procedure manual. He mentioned "teaching" and "baptizing," but He never spelled out any exact styles, approaches, or tools. Why? Because He was intense about involvement but relaxed regarding method. He wants us to actively reach out to others, but the way we do it depends on the

---

3. Gerhard Kittel and Gerhard Friedrich, eds., *Theological Dictionary of the New Testament,* translated and abridged in one volume by Geoffrey W. Bromiley (1985; reprint, Grand Rapids, Mich.: William B. Eerdmans Publishing Co., 1992), pp. 555, 560.

needs and personality of the people we're involved with. How we reach teenagers will be different from how we share the gospel with children. Migrant workers will need a different approach than the highly educated. Sensitivity is the key—we must respond to each individual's uniqueness, just as Jesus did.

4. Jesus Called for Action

Jesus' commission was never meant to simply be studied; it was a call to action. Look again at the verbs: "Go . . . make disciples . . . baptizing . . . teaching" (Matt. 28:19–20); "preach" (Mark 16:15); "be My witnesses" (Acts 1:8). Energy and movement pulse through these words.

God may not be calling you to become a full-time missionary, but He is challenging you to participate in His Great Commission. Does it feel a little overwhelming? Are you wondering where to begin? Jesus' words in Acts 1:8 will help us know how to start.

Where to Begin; Where to End

Before Jesus ascended to heaven, He told the disciples,

> "And you shall be My witnesses both in Jerusalem, and in all Judea and Samaria, and even to the remotest part of the earth." (Acts 1:8b)

Why did Jesus begin with Jerusalem? Because that was where the disciples would be, waiting to receive the Holy Spirit (vv. 4–5). In other words, He told them to begin where they were. Our Jerusalems, then, may be our families and friends. We start sharing the gospel where we live.

Jesus next mentioned Judea, the area surrounding Jerusalem. Judea was within the Jews' circle of comfort. They knew it well and worked and lived within its borders. Our equivalent would be the neighboring cities of our hometown, our county, and even our state.

Samaria, however, was definitely outside the disciples' comfort zone. That's where the Samaritans lived, who were of mixed Jewish-Gentile background—and who were treated with hostility by "pure" Jews. For us today, a Samaritan would be someone who challenges our prejudices—a person of another race or social strata. Our Samaria is a place we normally would not choose to go, a place God uses to stretch us and shape us in Christ's inclusive, all-encompassing love.

154

Finally, Christ mentions that the disciples should be His witnesses in "the remotest part of the earth." Literally, they should seek to cover the whole world with the gospel. Of course, this was an order too tall for those eleven men to accomplish in their lifetimes. Even today, the church, with nearly two thousand years of history filled with brave and courageous missionaries, has yet to accomplish the task. Yet we, like the disciples, should continue to strive to reach the remotest parts of the world until Christ returns. After all, this command was His final request, and we should honor Him by giving it the same priority He gave it.

Living Insights

The world is closer than you think. With just a click of a button, the Internet can take you anywhere in the world to meet people all around the globe. Satellite TV can put you in touch with international news. And even cable TV can bring you programs from Korea, Vietnam, India, France, Germany, Mexico, Taiwan, and China.

How can we turn this exposure to other cultures into direct interaction? Here are a few ideas.

- Invite a family from another culture over for dinner.

- Adopt one of the missionary families your church sponsors. Send them letters and care packages. Host them when they're in the area, and help your children develop friendships with their kids.

- Sponsor a child through a Christian relief organization such as Compassion International (1-800-336-7676; www.ci.org) or World Vision (1-888-511-6592; www.worldvision.org), or any other of your choice.

- House a foreign exchange student.

- Use your vacation time for a short-term missions trip.

- Read a book on missions involvement. We recommend Paul Borthwick's *How to Be a World-Class Christian* (Wheaton, Ill.: Scripture Press Publications, Victor Books, 1991).

- Get involved with a ministry to international students at a local college.

- Set aside some extra money each month to give directly to missions.

- Consider using your skills in another country. Mission organizations often need business managers, teachers, artisans, and computer programmers, to name a few.

What are some ways you can start fulfilling the Great Commission from where you live?

_____

_____

_____

_____

_____

Always, pray for the people you read about in the newspaper, on the Internet, or see on TV. God knows their names, even though you don't. Perhaps someday they'll become Christians because you touched their lives with prayer.

Chapter 20

WATCHING FOR JESUS IN THE AIR

1 Corinthians 15:50–57; 1 Thessalonians 4:13–18; Titus 2:11–13

No study about Jesus Christ would be complete without looking ahead to His imminent return—His Rapture of His church. Here's what He Himself said about it:

> "Do not let your heart be troubled; believe in God, believe also in Me. In My Father's house are many dwelling places; if it were not so, I would have told you; for I go to prepare a place for you. If I go and prepare a place for you, I will come again and receive you to Myself, that where I am, there you may be also." (John 14:1–3)

How comforting to know that Christ will come back for us! At least, it should be comforting. Is it for you? Or do you, like the Corinthian and Thessalonian believers, have some questions about it that trouble you? They wondered, What has happened to those who have already died? How will Christ come for them? What about non-Christians? What about those who will be alive when He returns?

Perhaps you've wondered about some of these same things yourself. Before we see how Paul answered these questions, let's first clarify two concepts that relate to all of them.

Two Clarifications concerning Death and Destiny

What happens when we die? Where do our souls go at the moment of our death? Two concepts lie beneath these questions—death and destiny.

Death

Death is not an ending. Rather, it's a separation. The soul—that invisible part of us that gives us life and personality—separates from our body. The body ceases to function—it dies—but the soul lives on without the body.

Destiny

Where does the soul go now that death has evicted it from its home? Scripture teaches us that the souls of believers go to live in the presence of the Lord (2 Cor. 5:8; Luke 16:22; 23:43). The souls of unbelievers, however, go to hades, also called hell—a place of suffering (Luke 16:22–23). Nowhere does Scripture teach the concept of purgatory. Rather, it teaches that a person's destiny is sealed upon death. We do not have the ability to go back or change our destinies once we've died.

Perishable Transformed into Imperishable

So, if Christ is coming back for all who believe in Him, both those still living and those who have died, what is He going to do about our perishable bodies, if anything? In 1 Corinthians 15:50–57, Paul reveals the answer to this "mystery." This is not a mystery in the sense of being hard to understand or enigmatic. Rather, it's a reality that is hidden to the uninitiated—a secret. And it's a secret he wants all Christians in on.

Answering an Underlying Question

Paul has already explained in 1 Corinthians 15:35–49 that the dead in Christ will be raised and has described the nature of their resurrection bodies. But what about those who are still alive on that resurrection day? Will they remain in their earthly bodies? This must have weighed heavily on the Corinthian believers' minds. So Paul supplies the answer, beginning in verse 50.

> Now I say this, brethren, that flesh and blood cannot inherit the kingdom of God; nor does the perishable inherit the imperishable.

Simply stated, nothing perishable is equipped to endure eternity. Therefore, even those who are alive when Christ comes for us will receive new bodies. This is the mystery Paul wants us to understand:

> Behold, I tell you a mystery; we will not all sleep, but we will all be changed. (v. 51)

Those who have died will be resurrected to receive their new bodies, and then those still living will get their new bodies as well. Is this a long, gradual process? Not at all, as Paul explains next.

The Suddenness of Our Transformation

Our transformation from perishable to imperishable will occur suddenly. Paul says it will happen "in a moment, in the twinkling of an eye" (v. 52a). The Greek term for *moment*, *atomos*, means "uncut" or "indivisible because of smallness"; and the phrase for "in the twinkling of an eye," *en ripe opthalmou*, conveys the same idea as the English phrase "in the blink of an eye."[1]

How It Will Occur

What will signal this sudden event? Paul describes that next:

> For the trumpet will sound, and the dead will be
> raised imperishable, and we will be changed. (v. 52b)

In 1 Thessalonians, which we'll examine more closely later in this chapter, Paul adds that an angel will shout prior to the trumpet blast. So, the order of events for the Rapture will be as follows:

- An angel will shout,
- a trumpet will be heard,
- the dead believers will be raised first,
- and then the living will be changed.

Whether living or dead, however, *all* will be transformed.

The Need to Be Transformed

Paul reiterates the necessity of transformation prior to entering God's presence:

> For this perishable must put on the imperishable,
> and this mortal must put on immortality. (v. 53)

Perishable flesh simply cannot mix with God's immortal kingdom; so we not only will be changed—we *must* be changed. Then something grand will occur.

Victory over Death!

Our transformation at the Rapture not only gives us immortal

---

1. Gordon D. Fee, *The First Epistle to the Corinthians*, The New International Commentary on the New Testament series (Grand Rapids, Mich.: William B. Eerdmans Publishing Co., 1987), p. 801.

life but also defeats death:

> But when this perishable will have put on the imperishable, and this mortal will have put on immortality, then will come about the saying that is written, "Death is swallowed up in victory. O death, where is your victory? O death, where is your sting?" The sting of death is sin, and the power of sin is the law; but thanks be to God, who gives us the victory through our Lord Jesus Christ. (vv. 54–57)

When we are made new in Christ, our age-old enemy, death, will be the conquered, not the conqueror. Death will stalk us no more, cause no more pain and sorrow. Commentators Curtis Vaughan and Thomas D. Lea tell us that "in speaking of the 'sting' of death, the apostle depicts death as a venomous serpent inflicting fatal wounds. Christ, however, has drawn its sting and left it powerless."[2] Thanks be to God, indeed, for graciously allowing us to share in Christ's victory over death! As William Barclay reflected, Christ

> came to tell us that God is not law, but love, that the centre of God's being is not legalism but grace, that we go out, not to a judge, but to a Father who awaits his children coming home. Because of that Jesus gave us victory over death, its fear banished in the wonder of God's love.[3]

Be Informed . . . Be Comforted

As a result of Paul's teachings on the Rapture, some first-century believers reacted in extremes. The Thessalonian church was particularly plagued by this problem. Ecstatic about Christ's imminent return and their transformation, some Thessalonian believers quit their jobs and awaited the Rapture in idleness.[4] Also troubling the church was a lot of misinformation. The people were afraid their departed loved ones would be forgotten by Christ when He returned.

2. Curtis Vaughan and Thomas D. Lea, 1 Corinthians, Bible Study Commentary series (Grand Rapids, Mich.: Zondervan Publishing House, Lamplighter Books, 1983), p. 164.

3. William Barclay, The Letters to the Corinthians, rev. ed., The Daily Study Bible Series (Philadelphia, Pa.: Westminster Press, 1975), p. 160.

4. This section has been adapted from the study guide Contagious Christianity: A Study of 1 Thessalonians, coauthored by Bryce Klabunde, from the Bible-teaching ministry of Charles R. Swindoll (Anaheim, Calif.: Insight for Living, 1993), pp. 63–65.

So Paul, in his first letter to them, gave them a detailed explanation.

Regarding Our Death and Life Afterwards

Affirming the need for Christians to understand these truths, Paul begins:

> We do not want you to be uninformed, brethren, about those who are asleep. (1 Thess. 4:13a)

Asleep is a euphemism for death, minus the finality. It is a hopeful word, because sleeping assumes a future "awakening"—a resurrection. Motivating Paul's words is his pastoral concern "that you will not grieve as do the rest who have no hope" (v. 13b).

Paul says we don't have to grieve without hope. Notice, however, that he doesn't say we're not supposed to grieve. Don't let people tell you that strong Christians don't weep when death claims a loved one. The fact is, not until we experience the emotional depths of grief can we step into life's fullness again. We must "walk *through* the valley of the shadow of death" before we can reach the other side (Ps. 23:4a, emphasis added). But through that valley, God is by our side, reminding us of the eternal sunshine beyond the grieving and the grave.

The basis of our hope is that "Jesus died and rose again" (1 Thess. 4:14a)—the most significant statement in Scripture. Through His atoning sacrifice and His grave-defeating resurrection, Christ has conquered sin and death. As a result,

> if we believe that Jesus died and rose again, even so God will bring with Him those who have fallen asleep in Jesus. (v. 14)

There's that word again, *asleep*. As Paul unfolds the subject of the resurrection and Rapture, he makes it clear that God will arouse the sleeping bodies of dead believers.

Regarding Christ's Coming and Others' Joining

Paul next sets out the order of events surrounding the resurrection, this time including the Rapture too.

> For this we say to you by the word of the Lord, that we who are alive and remain until the coming of the Lord, will not precede those who have fallen asleep. For the Lord Himself will descend from

161

heaven with a shout, with the voice of the archangel and with the trumpet of God, and the dead in Christ will rise first. Then we who are alive and remain will be caught up together with them in the clouds to meet the Lord in the air, and so we shall always be with the Lord. (vv. 15–17)

We, like the Thessalonians, have nothing to fear concerning our loved ones who have died in Christ. They will be the first Christ gathers to Himself. Then those who are alive will follow. What a family reunion that will be! Husbands and wives, parents and children, friends and relatives separated by death will join hands once again to live forever, together with Christ.

Regarding Confidence and Comfort

"Therefore," Paul concludes, "comfort one another with these words" (v. 18). His words are for the fearful, who wonder if Christ has forgotten the dead; for the unsure, who wonder what lies beyond the grave; and for the grieving, who think the last rose on the coffin must be the final good-bye. Christ has not forgotten, eternal life is free, and death is only sleep. These words inspire confidence and hope.

Responding to Christ's Coming

In light of what we've learned, we must ask ourselves, "What does it mean to prepare for Christ's coming? How do I respond to this?" Paul provides direction in a letter to his friend Titus:

> For the grace of God has appeared, bringing salvation to all men, instructing us to deny ungodliness and worldly desires and to live sensibly, righteously and godly in the present age, looking for the blessed hope and the appearing of the glory of our great God and Savior, Christ Jesus. (Titus 2:11–13)

From this passage, we can draw four practical responses. First, *make certain you have taken what God has given—His salvation.* Christ died to pay for your sins and rose to give you eternal life. To be forgiven and to receive life, He asks simply that you place your belief in Him. Have you?

Second, *continue to resist a corrupt lifestyle.* Paul instructs us to "deny ungodliness and worldly desires" so we won't be caught unprepared. Are you?

Third, *live in a sensible, godly manner.* Live as if Christ might come today. Stay involved in Christ's program; give yourself to the Savior; share His love with others. Do you?

Fourth, *from now on, keep watching for Jesus in the air.* Like a child on Christmas Eve, anticipate His coming and the gifts He will bring. Remind yourself of the "blessed hope" to come. Will you?

Living Insights

What can we do to prepare for the Lord's coming? Let's look through the following Scriptures to discover some ways to keep focusing heavenward.

According to the following verses, what benefits await Christians at Christ's coming?

2 Corinthians 5:1–5 _____

_____

1 Peter 1:3–5 _____

_____

What should be our attitudes toward Christ's coming?

Philippians 3:20 _____

_____

2 Timothy 4:8 _____

_____

What attitudes and actions characterize those who are keeping ready?

Romans 13:11–14 _____

_____

Philippians 4:5 _____

_____

James 5:8–9 _____

_____

1 Peter 4:7–11 _____

_____

Suppose Christ told you that He was planning to come at midnight tomorrow. How would that knowledge affect your relationship with God?

_____

_____

_____

How would it affect the way you relate to others?

_____

_____

_____

How would it affect the way you feel about yourself?

_____

_____

_____

Christ could come tomorrow at midnight. He may even come before you finish reading this sentence. What changes should you make to better prepare for the resurrection and Rapture?

_____

_____

_____

_____

BOOKS FOR
PROBING FURTHER

How can we possibly take in all the richness of God's majestic Son in twenty short studies? It isn't possible! Christ is too vast, too deep, too profound to be contained in one guide or book. So, to help you discover more about our Lord and grow deeper in your love for Him, we have provided the following list of books.

Flynn, Leslie B. *The Miracles of Jesus*. Wheaton, Ill.: Scripture Press Publications, Victor Books, 1990.

Gariepy, Henry. *100 Portraits of Christ*. Wheaton, Ill.: Scripture Press Publications, Victor Books, 1993.

Gire, Ken. *Intimate Moments with the Savior: Learning to Love*. Grand Rapids, Mich.: Zondervan Publishing House, 1989.

———. *Incredible Moments with the Savior: Learning to See*. Grand Rapids, Mich.: Zondervan Publishing House, 1990.

———. *Instructive Moments with the Savior: Learning to Hear*. Grand Rapids, Mich.: Zondervan Publishing House, 1992.

———. *Intense Moments with the Savior: Learning to Feel*. Grand Rapids, Mich.: Zondervan Publishing House, 1994.

Kaiser, Walter C., Jr. *The Messiah in the Old Testament*. Grand Rapids, Mich.: Zondervan Publishing House, 1995.

Lucado, Max. *And the Angels Were Silent: The Final Week of Jesus*. Sisters, Ore.: Multnomah Publishers, 1999.

Miller, Calvin. *Once upon a Tree*. 2d ed. Grand Rapids, Mich.: Baker Book House, 1991.

Miller, Calvin, ed. *The Book of Jesus: A Treasury of the Greatest Stories and Writings about Christ*. Rev. ed. New York, N.Y.: Simon and Schuster, Touchstone Books, 1998.

Morris, Leon. *The Atonement: Its Meaning and Significance*. 1983. Reprint, Downers Grove, Ill.: InterVarsity Press, 1984.

Olford, Stephen F. *Living Words and Loving Deeds: Messages on Christ's*

Claims and Miracles in the Gospel of John. Grand Rapids, Mich.: Baker Book House, 1992.

Pentecost, J. Dwight. *The Words and Works of Jesus Christ.* Grand Rapids, Mich.: Zondervan Publishing House, 1981.

Sanders, J. Oswald. *The Incomparable Christ: The Person and Work of Jesus Christ.* Rev. and enl. ed. Chicago, Ill.: Moody Press, 1971.

Simpson, A. B. *Christ in the Tabernacle.* Camp Hill, Pa.: Christian Publications, 1985.

———. *The Names of Jesus.* Camp Hill, Pa.: Christian Publications, 1991.

Sproul, R. C. *The Glory of Christ.* Wheaton, Ill.: Tyndale House Publishers, 1990.

Stott, John R. W. *The Cross of Christ.* Downers Grove, Ill.: Inter-Varsity Press, 1986.

Wangerin, Walter, Jr. *Reliving the Passion: Meditations on the Suffering, Death and Resurrection of Jesus as Recorded in Mark.* Grand Rapids, Mich.: Zondervan Publishing House, 1992.

Yancey, Philip. *The Jesus I Never Knew.* Grand Rapids, Mich.: Zondervan Publishing House, 1995.

Some of these books may be out of print and available only through a library. For those currently available, please contact your local Christian bookstore. Books by Charles R. Swindoll, as well as some books by other authors, may be obtained through Insight for Living.

Insight for Living also offers study guides on many books of the Bible, as well as on a variety of issues and biblical personalities. For more information, see the ordering instructions that follow and contact the office that serves you.

NOTES

NOTES

NOTES

NOTES

ORDERING INFORMATION

THE MAJESTY OF GOD'S SON

If you would like to order additional study guides, purchase the cassette series that accompanies this guide, or request our product catalogs, please contact the office that serves you.

United States and International locations:

Insight for Living
Post Office Box 69000
Anaheim, CA 92817-0900

1-800-772-8888, 24 hours a day, seven days a week
(714) 575-5000, 8:00 A.M. to 4:30 P.M., Pacific time, Monday to Friday

Canada:

Insight for Living Ministries
Post Office Box 2510
Vancouver, BC, Canada V6B 3W7

1-800-663-7639, 24 hours a day, seven days a week

Australia:

Insight for Living, Inc.
General Post Office Box 2823 EE
Melbourne, VIC 3001, Australia

Toll-free 1800-772-888 or (03) 9877-4277, 8:30 A.M. to 5:00 P.M., Monday to Friday

World Wide Web:

www.insight.org

Study Guide Subscription Program

Study guide subscriptions are available. Please call or write the office nearest you to find out how you can receive our study guides on a regular basis.